magic house

magic house

practical magic for a harmonious home

TERESA MOOREY

RYLAND
PETERS
& SMALL

LONDON NEW YORK

SENIOR DESIGNER Paul Tilby
SENIOR EDITOR Clare Double
LOCATION AND PICTURE RESEARCH MANAGER Claire Hector
PRODUCTION Patricia Harrington
ART DIRECTOR Gabriella Le Grazie
PUBLISHING DIRECTOR Alison Starling

EDITORIAL CONSULTANT Christina Rodenbeck

The author would like to thank Lorraine Rustell
for some of the ideas used in this book.

First published in the United States
in 2003 by Ryland Peters & Small, Inc.
519 Broadway, 5th Floor
New York NY 10012
www.rylandpeters.com

10 9 8 7 6 5 4 3 2 1

Printed and bound in China

Library of Congress Cataloging-in-Publication Data
Moorey, Teresa.
  Magic house : practical magic for a harmonious home /
Teresa Moorey.--
1st US ed.
     p. cm.
Includes bibliographical references and index.
  ISBN 1-84172-484-X
1. Magic. 2. Home--Miscellanea. 3. Households--
Miscellanea. 4. Witchcraft. I. Title.
  BF1623.H67M66 2003
  133.4'3--dc21
                        2003008485

Do not use essential oils neat or take them internally. The
publishers cannot accept liability for any injury, damage,
or loss to person or property, direct or inconsequential,
arising from suggestions made in this book.

Contents

Introduction

MAKE ME A WILLOW CABIN AT YOUR GATE,
AND CALL UPON MY SOUL WITHIN THE HOUSE
WILLIAM SHAKESPEARE, *Twelfth Night*

Your house is more than a home for your body—it is a shrine for your spirit. From nest to temple, pad to palace, it not only contains, but cultivates. Your dwelling can be lovingly arranged and decorated to uplift you, soothe you, stimulate you, and entrance you. Each room can be a theater for magic, lending itself and the objects it contains to specific charms. As you will discover, many ordinary things in your home have magical uses. Your home's ambience will be enhanced by well-chosen and beautiful items that you also use for spells.

The existence of a spirit of place has long been recognized. Every location has its special, subtle characteristics. Some of these, such as scent or the fall of light, may be obvious to our five ordinary senses, but others can only be apprehended by our instincts. In this book you will discover a simple way to detect the "energy-patterns" in your home, by dowsing. More than this, you will find many ways to conjure the effects you desire upon yourself, your family, friends, and pets. Some of these will be obvious, such as choice of color to generate mood. Others will be much more magical, drawing upon ancient beliefs and traditional teachings. Wise and practical householders are realizing today that much has been lost in the stress of modern life, and they are drawing on old ways to bring heart and soul back to their domestic surroundings.

The Chinese system of feng shui teaches that an unseen energy, chi, flows within and around us. It states that space within the home has symbolic value. I will draw on feng shui, as well as other traditions, so you can enhance your environment in the best way for you. Much is a matter of common sense and instinct. In your magical house, both your intuition and your practical capabilities will be fostered, to work at their smoothest.

Your home is your haven and delight, to be creatively adorned so it can urge your personality to flower. Tend it with love—and a touch of magic!

Your Magical Toolkit

More Than Bricks and Mortar

Cultures all over the world recognize that space is sacred. The point upon the Earth where we find ourselves is the center of our consciousness, and so has a magical quality. The place we define as our home also houses our soul, and can be designed so that we blossom.

Western traditions describe four elements: Earth, Air, Fire, and Water. These are not only the four states of matter; they have endless symbolism. See the table opposite for the most important of these symbols. All the elements need to be represented in our homes if we are to feel vibrant and balanced. Fire is the most lacking in the modern home—hence the popularity of candles.

These four elements are also represented in Native American culture, as part of the Medicine Wheel. "Medicine" means power, and this "power wheel" is a representation of the cosmos—and the home—in balance. Animals represent the elements. You could create a wheel in your home, using animal ornaments, wherever you feel you need a power-center.

In contrast, the Chinese have five elements: Earth, Fire, Metal, Wood, and Water. More than one system is valid in the unseen worlds. What matters is what appeals to you—and what works. Feng shui, the "magical" arrangement of space, states that different areas of the home correlate to specific areas of life. Thus, making a change in an area of your dwelling can also change that aspect of your life.

YOUR OWN HOUSEHOLD GODS

There is a host of gods, talismans, charms, special plants, and lucky customs designed to entice fortune home. The Romans had their lares, or household gods, to whom they brought offerings at the start of May. One of the most popular Chinese gods is Tsao Chun, the Kitchen God. In the week before New Year he is especially honored, for legend states that now he returns to heaven to report on the family! In the British Isles, certain trees, such as rowan and hawthorn, are said to protect the home, and a horseshoe over the door is thought lucky. You also have your talismans. They may be family portraits or childhood toys. These things affect you—are they not magical? Think about how to give them pride of place in your home.

TABLE OF THE ELEMENTS

TRADITION	ELEMENT	SYMBOLISM
Western	EARTH	Protection, solidity, and common sense
	AIR	Clear thought, communication, and study
	FIRE	Inspiration, courage, and passion
	WATER	Healing, reflection, and cleansing
Native American examples (there are many different systems)	EARTH	Bear
	AIR	Buffalo (or other animals that sweep over vast distances)
	FIRE	Eagle
	WATER	Dolphin
Chinese	EARTH	Yin/yang symbol, moderation, and balance
	FIRE	Red phoenix, joy, and hope
	METAL	White tiger, unpredictability, and power
	WOOD	Green dragon, wisdom, and protection
	WATER	Black tortoise, mystery, ritual, and nurture

Organizing Your Box of Tricks

THE LITTLE THINGS ARE INFINITELY THE MOST IMPORTANT

Sir Arthur Conan Doyle, *The Adventures of Sherlock Holmes*

To work your domestic wizardry you will need a few basic items. If you can, choose things you find attractive, and store or display them with care. This will make you feel especially good about using them. If possible, keep them in a special decorated box or small cupboard that will also make a lovely addition to your home.

Here is your checklist. Remember, you can pick and choose—you can adapt and modify your magical toolbox until it feels right for you.

Candles in as many shapes, sizes, and colors as you like. Candles are used in many spells, in candlesticks, glass goblets, lanterns, or whatever you wish; you probably have plenty of suitable holders already.

Incense sticks or powdered incense. If you choose the latter, you will need a holder to burn it in, and charcoal.

Oil burner and essential oils, as appropriate.

A chalice and/or bowl to hold water for certain spells.

A selection of semi-precious stones and crystals to use when you wish. You can buy these at reasonable cost from New Age stores.

A **crystal pendant** to use in dowsing.

A besom. This twiggy broom is a large item that can be displayed, if you have space, in your kitchen or by your hearth. It speaks of magic, traditional ways, and flights of the spirit.

A special blunt knife or wand. When you perform certain spells, you can surround yourself with a magic circle made of "mind-stuff" to contain the energy until you are ready. Use the knife or wand to create your circle symbolically. Your knife may be ornate or ordinary, but reserve it for magic. Similarly, your wand may be a piece of fallen wood you picked up or something decorated and jeweled. If you create a circle, always remember to will it away when your spell is done.

Salt in a special bowl.

A notebook for spells, so you know what you've done, when, and why!

Knife or scissors to cut herbs.

Bell or gong.

Calendar of the Moon's phases.

Special effigies, animal, god or goddess figures, and good-luck charms that are important to you.

Colored scarves or cloths.

Colored threads.

Herbs and spices, as necessary.

A robe, if you wish.

Where possible, rub or sprinkle salt on items before you use them, as a symbolic cleansing. Light an incense stick or some powdered incense, and circle the item three times, dedicating it to love, peace, and joy. Now you're ready to go!

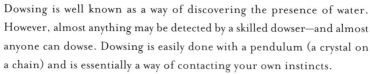

Domestic Dowsing

**HEARD MELODIES ARE SWEET, BUT THOSE UNHEARD
ARE SWEETER**

JOHN KEATS, *Ode on a Grecian Urn*

Dowsing is well known as a way of discovering the presence of water. However, almost anything may be detected by a skilled dowser—and almost anyone can dowse. Dowsing is easily done with a pendulum (a crystal on a chain) and is essentially a way of contacting your own instincts.

Hold the chain of a newly cleansed pendulum and let the crystal dangle until it starts to swing (see box opposite). Say **" Show me 'yes',"** and watch the movement, which is usually clockwise. Do the same for "no." Test these responses against something you know—for instance, hold your crystal over a bowl of water and ask, **" Is this water?"**. When you have done this several times, you will feel confident enough to use your crystal.

Now you are ready to discover the hidden energy-patterns in your house. Ask your pendulum to show you where the energies are strongest by indicating "yes" in those areas. When you discover energized spots, ask if they are good or bad. Plot lines of energy going through your house by noticing where the pendulum reacts, whether any straight line formations are emerging, and so on. If you discover bad energies, they may be neutralized by placing a copper coil under the floor or the carpet. If the vibes are good, find out in what way—for example, for creativity, love-making, meditation—by a process of elimination.

You can dowse specific objects to find out what you need to know. For instance, is a certain food good for you? Dangle the pendulum over it and ask. Is a plant healthy? Is an essential oil therapeutic? Let the swing of the crystal help you decide. Your crystal can become your domestic companion—beautiful, as well as true!

FINDING A PENDULUM

Choose a fairly large crystal, over
¾ inch (2 cm) long if possible, and
lozenge-shaped. Cleanse it in spring
water and imagine negativity leaving
it. You may need to do this regularly if your crystal is
on display in a busy room. Admire your crystal, watch it
by moonlight and candlelight until you feel a bond
with it. Your crystal will serve as an ornament when
not in use, hanging in your window and casting small
rainbows around the room as the Sun catches it.

TRUST YOUR INTUITION

Most dowsers accept, quite happily,
that they are moving the pendulum
themselves. The point is that the
subconscious mind causes these
little tremors, not the conscious
one. And so the movement of the
pendulum can tell you what your
intuition already knows, deep down.

Your Domestic Altar

HAVE YOU PEACE, THE QUIET URGE THAT REVEALS YOUR POWER?

KAHLIL GIBRAN, *THE PROPHET*

Your home needs a sacred space to act as its spiritual focus. This will be both a shrine to whatever spirituality is meaningful to you and also a working area that you can use for certain spells: your domestic altar.

If you have a room you can put aside as sacred space, so much the better. It will offer a peaceful and comfortable place to meditate and do magic. However, you can achieve just the same effect on a smaller scale.

Your altar is best sited in the heart of your home, away from drafts but well-lit and accessible. A sturdy shelf, out of reach of children and animals, is a good idea. Make your altar beautiful, so you love to look at it. Drape it with colorful fabric if you wish, and give pride of place to something special. This may well be a god or goddess figure, a large crystal, a sculpture, or anything that has symbolic meaning for you and will act as a benign presence in your house.

On each side of the altar place candles, in candlesticks. These can be lit on special occasions, at seasonal times (see "A Home for All Seasons," pages 100–115) or at Full or Dark Moon. Change the colors of your candles to suit the occasion or time of year. You can also mark the passage of the seasons on your altar, for instance with a bowl of russet leaves in fall. This makes your home in harmony with the rhythms of Nature.

A vase of flowers is another offering idea. Make sure you tend your altar regularly, ensuring the bouquet is fresh and vibrant. A decorated chalice, symbolic of the womb and the creative energies of your home, may be used as a vase, or left empty. Amulets such as corn dollies or love-spoons can be placed alongside. Encourage family members to take part in decorating the altar, each using it in a way both personal to them and keeping the whole household in mind. Acting in this manner in itself constitutes a spell for domestic solidarity. You may find guests bring their own offerings, both as a blessing and to take part in the bounty of your domestic sphere.

You may also wish to have a permanent censer, incense-stick holder, or oil burner on your altar. For a true ambience of the sacred, keep an eternal flame burning as a night light, secured within a covered lantern.

Come In, Lady Moon

I SEE THE MOON
AND THE MOON SEES ME
GOD BLESS THE MOON
AND GOD BLESS ME

NURSERY RHYME

The Moon is Queen of Dreams and your home wants to breathe in her enchantment. From the blood in your veins to the bricks in your house, all is affected by the Moon, and responds to her ebb and flow. Welcoming in the Moon encourages your intuition to blossom and helps you attune to your needs and those of your family.

The phases of the Moon are listed in most newspapers. Full Moon is a more "happening" time while Dark Moon, when she isn't visible, is better for meditation and rest. Take a note of your own responses, for they may vary.

When the first bright sickle of the New Moon appears in the evening sky, place silver candles on your altar. Change these to large, white candles when she is Full; dark blue or black are best to mark the end of the cycle. A white crystal could represent Full Moon, and onyx or apache tear represent the Dark or waning Moon.

Magnify the light of the Full Moon by catching her reflection in a mirror, and use it to meditate and expand your creativity. Make notes in a silver-backed notebook or with a silver pen. Water is the lunar element, so place a large bowl of water on your windowsill to catch the Moon's shimmering face.

You can celebrate Dark Moon by burning myrrh or patchouli incense and lighting a candle in a dark bowl. Watch the smoke spiraling upwards and reflect on the new phase just beginning. Take part in this transitional quiet time by spreading a dark blue or purple throw on a bed or chair and sitting by candlelight to savor the peace and promise of the shadows.

LUNAR STRESS RELIEF

If your life is stressful, you may especially cherish the peaceful, yin effect of the Moon. Create this at all times by choosing silver ornaments, operating by candlelight whenever possible, installing a large, hypnotic fishtank, and filling your home with fragrant white blooms. Lilies, with their heady sweetness, are ruled by the Moon. Owls, bats, wolves, dogs, snakes, and dolphins are some creatures linked with the Moon because of their habits or habitat. You can add them to your home as ornaments.

MOON IMAGERY

Pictures of the Moon, such as "Weary Moon" by Edward Robert Hughes, add a dreamy feel to bedrooms. Grays, violets, soft blues, and purples are the lunar palette—use them when and where you wish, to loosen up and go inwards, but avoid them in rooms where you have to be active or sociable. Lunar ornaments, such as crescent-shaped plaques and candle holders, bring a hint of lunar secrets.

Space Harmony

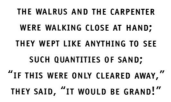

THE WALRUS AND THE CARPENTER
WERE WALKING CLOSE AT HAND;
THEY WEPT LIKE ANYTHING TO SEE
SUCH QUANTITIES OF SAND;
"IF THIS WERE ONLY CLEARED AWAY,"
THEY SAID, "IT WOULD BE GRAND!"

LEWIS CARROLL, *THROUGH THE LOOKING GLASS*

If you frequently lose things at home and feel confused and irritated, then your clutter level is too high for you. You need to bring some space harmony into your home. Remember that each person's definition of clutter may be different. To the minimalist, everything unnecessary is ugly. To someone who prefers a lived-in look, belongings lying about are cozy. So you need to decide how much clutter you genuinely like—as opposed to put up with out of laziness—and what works for you.

Start your clutter-busting by clearing your mind. You will need some lavender oil, a light blue candle, a crystal glass filled with water, and any substance that can be sprinkled in the water to cloud it, and then go clear. (Try table salt or baking soda.)

Light the candle and say, **"I cast light into dusty corners."**

Anoint your wrists and forehead with lavender oil, saying, **"I am calm, methodical, and steady."**

Now place the substance in the water. Watch it clear and say, **"As this water clears, so does my mind, and as my mind, my house."**

Keep the candle burning, and some lavender oil handy to apply when needed. Now start sorting out your clutter. Begin small—one cupboard, one collection; years of accumulation won't disappear in an hour. Sort storage space first, to make room for the stuff you have lying around, for that is more likely to be useful than what hasn't seen daylight for years. As you sort, remember that clutter can be an emotional issue. Your attachment to dingy possessions may mean you cannot let go of the past, but to move on in your life you must make room for better things. Be gentle with yourself, take frequent breaks and, as you apply the lavender, affirm to yourself that its fragrance is bringing you a brighter future.

Create three piles, one for throwing out or recycling, one for "not sure," and one for keeping. Anything you have not used for a year should probably go. Face the fact that you may regret some things, but you need the space more—for space is also a commodity. Your "not sure" pile should be the smallest, and can go in the attic, cellar, or garage. Get rid of unwanted items before you change your mind.

Reward yourself by arranging your kept items, lovingly, in their new-found space. How good they look, and how well you've done! Sprinkle a little lavender in the storage space and give yourself a treat. You deserve it.

Cleansing Your Home

A good cleansing is essential as soon as you move into a new home. Your home needs loving practical attention with vacuum cleaner and duster, followed by a magical "sweep out." This will get rid of any bad atmosphere or negativity left by the previous occupants. Do your usual clean, as thoroughly as you feel is necessary. Then it is time to concentrate on subtle matters.

Wearing your robe, if you wish, take your besom and begin sweeping out. Start with the uppermost room, furthest from the door. Swish the besom through the air, imagining any negative influences as clouds of smoke that you are chasing out through the door. When you feel this is complete, close the door to that room and proceed to the next, through all the upstairs rooms. Now do the same along the landing and down the stairs, and with each of the downstairs rooms in turn. Finally, sweep your collected smog out of the front door and close it.

Equip a tray with a lighted incense stick, a white candle, your special salt, and water in your chalice. If you prefer, take your censer instead of the incense stick, with an incense that contains rosemary. For a stronger effect, if you feel your home had questionable former occupants, include benzoin (gum benjamin), from herbal and aromatherapy stores. Other fragrant ingredients could be frankincense, copal, and sandalwood.

Go from room to room. Sprinkle salt, saying **" Be blessed by Earth;"** sprinkle water, saying **" Be blessed by Water;"** waft the incense, saying **"Be blessed by Air;"** and gently move the lighted candle around, saying **" Be blessed by Fire."** Finally, say **" Blessed Be"** and move on to the next room. Play music as you do this to help you concentrate and make it a pleasure, not a chore.

When your circuit of the house is complete, place the candle on your altar, until it has burned down, if possible. Place the incense, chalice, and salt here, too. After a day or so, empty the chalice outside and replace the other items in your "magic box."

MAGICAL CLEANUP

All or part of this ritual may be repeated from time to time to keep your home psychically fresh, especially after arguments, upsets, illness, or difficult guests. Incense clears the air, water brings healing, fire burns off pettiness, and salt brings things down to earth. In time, the simple activity of bringing out your magical mop and bucket will calm, soothe, and encourage you. And the atmosphere in your home will be beautifully clear and serene.

HOME PROTECTION SPELL

Your home is your castle, holding your loved ones, your precious possessions—and your privacy. Having cleansed your home, your next magical task is to protect it. A good spell will repel intruders, giving them a psychic "kick" if they approach. Having said this, don't forget to lock your door! Acting on the material plane as well, will make your spell stronger.

For this spell you will need a horseshoe—any will do, but the genuine article has a special charm. You also need patchouli oil, a pot of salt, and brown candles (these can be hard to find, so you can substitute any dark color, even black). Also, before you begin, think of a protective symbol—anything that means safety to you.

Light the candles on your altar and relax. Cast a magic circle around you with your special knife or wand. Take up your horseshoe, holding it with its horns pointing upwards, and anoint it with patchouli oil, chanting **"My house stands firm, my fortune is fair"** three times.

Place the horseshoe before you with the pot of salt within its horns and relax again. Now visualize your circle expanding outwards from the pot of salt, which is its center, further and further until it pops through the walls and surrounds your whole house in an invisible bubble. Affirm very strongly that this bubble is there, that it keeps out anything bad but magnetizes good things, such as friendship.

Now imagine the bubble topped by your protective symbol, shining, pulsating, powerful. Take your salt and horseshoe and go over the entire house, placing a little salt on every external opening—windows, doors, attic entrances, toilets, sinks, airvents—anything that connects with outside. Imagine a smaller version of your protective symbol at each of these points—draw it in the air with your finger, wand, or knife, if you like.

Now go around the outside of the house, sprinkling salt wherever you can. If you live in a row house or apartment, some of this will have to be internal. Finally, fix your horseshoe over the front door, preferably outside.

Give thanks to any god or goddess that is special to you and ask them to watch over your home. Affirm that any traces of your magic circle have faded from the interior, and clap your hands to clear the air—but leave the external bubble intact.

When you've finished, why not toast your efforts and the powers that are helping you? Repeat parts of this ritual when you feel it is necessary.

A Journey Through Your Home

First Impressions

First impressions count, and your front door creates expectations about your home. It should welcome you, in particular, so consider your own preferences before those of visitors. Should the path be wide and open, or do you like seclusion? The color of your door is important, too. Mine is red and, although this is challenging, I find it cheery. Think about what you find appealing.

A porch offers shelter as you find your keys, and is a place to hang windchimes and decorative windmills. These keep the air nearby fresh and mobile, and attract activity in the form of visitors, mail, and deliveries. Don't be afraid of the obvious—a mat with "Welcome" on it offers just that! Before you even put your key in the door, the approach to your home will offer you welcome, safety—and some magical protection.

PLANT PROTECTION

Some plants are traditionally thought to increase your home's security. Make sure your front door is sturdy, then place one of these nearby.

BAY Bay, like holly, has long been considered a potent charm against evil spirits and wishes, as well as lightning and poison.

BRIGHT FLOWERS Chrysanthemums, geraniums, hyacinths, marigolds, and primroses all offer protective vibes and a splash of color.

HAWTHORN A hawthorn hedge is a great psychic barrier. You can also carry a twig to fight off depression, but it is unlucky to take it indoors.

HOLLY Holly has similar properties to bay, and is especially useful for entrances because it can be grown in a pot.

HONEYSUCKLE This is particularly lucky growing over your door and was believed to keep fevers at bay.

LAVENDER Lavender bushes yield up their scent when brushed, ensuring that all who come to your door feel calm and at ease.

ROWAN If you have room, a graceful rowan tree is especially fortunate. In olden times, house timbers made of rowan were inscribed with magical runes so all might be safe within.

A Magical Hallway

Your hallway is the "first kiss" your home offers—make sure it is seductive, and everyone will want more!

Scent is important because it awakens the senses. Well-placed potpourri means the first thing you smell is sweet. A vase of lilies or a dab of essential oil on a lampshade would also do the trick. You can buy earthenware rings to fit over the lightbulb in a lamp; drop fragrant oil onto the ring to heat when the lamp is switched on.

As you open your door, the first thing that hits your eye sets the tone. Choose pictures with great care. What do they symbolize? What emotions do they invoke? Of what do they remind you? All this should be in keeping with the general "feel" you expect from your home.

Make sure the hallway is clear, for this immediately assures you that all is orderly within. If it is small, keep it free of furniture and hang coats elsewhere.

Chinese wisdom teaches that stairs should not run straight towards the door. If yours do, break the headlong flow of chi with a windchime, or hang a small, decorative mirror on the inside of your door. Plants add to the vibrancy and welcome of your hall, but should not trail over the space. A luxurious rug or seat promises comfort and ease in store; a lamp offers gentle welcome. Relax and let your home enfold you.

> Place small pieces of sandalwood under the stair-carpet in several places, to keep your stairs safe. Sandalwood clears the air of negativity and offers your home protection.

> Keep a little jar containing flaxseed and red pepper near the door to prevent evil entering your home. If you wish, keep a candle nearby to light occasionally while you sprinkle a few seeds near the mat for extra care.

SAFEGUARD YOUR KEYS SPELL

Your doorkey is more than just a plain old tool to let you in. It symbolizes many other things such as security, belonging, ownership, and having an answer to life's problems—for that answer is your home. Protect your precious keys from loss or theft with this spell.

You will need a white candle, essential oils of patchouli and lavender, and some natural vanilla extract. You also need a very small hazel twig, a rowan twig, some red thread, and your favorite goddess or god effigy to watch over you. Hazel and rowan are both traditionally ruled by Mercury, as are keys themselves, for Mercury is the god of communication and travel, who can pass anywhere. They also lend wisdom and protection.

Light your candle and anoint both twigs and your key with the oils and vanilla extract, saying three times:

This rightful key to me I bind,
Intruders' eyes to it are blind.

Bind the twigs at right angles with the thread and attach the little cross you've made to your keyring. If this isn't practical, hang it on a hook where you also hang your keys. Place the keys on your domestic altar for one night in front of your god or goddess figure, asking for their blessing. Let the candle burn down if you can.

May your keys be blessed!

NEW MOON MONEY SPELL

To attract money, have a green doormat, if possible. The waxing Moon is favorable for all spells involving increase, and money is especially blessed by the New Moon. Look out for the first silver sliver of Moon in the evening sky and when you see her, take a silver coin, a gold coin, and the largest bill you can afford to invest. Place these on a south-facing windowsill, with the window open, so the Moon can "see" them without glass intervening. Burn some jasmine incense or a jasmine incense stick. Say:

Kindly Moon, as you grow, see great riches my way flow.
Watching Moon, more and more money comes in through my door.

Place all the money underneath your doormat and let the incense stick or powdered incense burn down in your hallway. Leave the money there until Full Moon. During this time, money should keep coming to you. Remove the bill and coins while the Moon is waning, but keep them safe and replace them next New Moon. Repeat the ceremony, if you feel it is necessary!

MOTHER NATURE'S LUCKY CHARM

For general good fortune, you need a holey-stone—a stone with a hole worn in it by water. These are sacred to the Great Mother, the Goddess of Nature, because the hole represents the womb of life from which all things come. If you can't obtain a holey-stone, use a substitute or make one yourself out of clay that hardens without firing. Wash your stone in a stream, visualizing it being cleansed of anything negative. Rub it with cinnamon oil (or you can substitute ground cinnamon). As you do this, imagine all kinds of good luck coming to your door. Finish off by holding the stone between your palms and projecting warmth and happiness into it. The holey-stone is now a lodestone for good fortune. Thread some green ribbon through it and hang it over or close to your front door. Take it down and recharge it every so often, especially at Full Moon, by cleansing it again and repeating the spell.

The Heart of the Home

Your living room is the place where the family comes together to relax away from the external hustle and bustle. It should be still and safe, but lively and stimulating at the same time, comfortable, and beautiful. This should be a room that no one wants to leave!

Clutter is disturbing to the eye, and thronged ornaments are no exception—choose one or two focal points such as a special vase or painting, and feature them in a soft spotlight. It is a good idea to change these periodically, as after a while you cease to appreciate their appeal.

LET THERE BE LIGHT

Lighting is important in creating your living room ambience. Try several soft side lights, and consider using colored bulbs. Pink is calming and satisfies a need for affection, red and orange are both heartening. Lights that can be angled will enable a serious reader to see their page while leaving others to chill out in half-light.

CREATE A TALKING STICK

Next to your hearth place a "talking stick." In tribal gatherings, the person who holds the stick claims the attention of the assembled folk, so use yours for important discussions. Like a magician's wand, with it in hand you conjure with words and send forth stirring power. As we talk, a kind of magic takes place within us, for often we aren't quite sure about something until we have framed it in words. A much-used talking stick carries the vibes of important announcements and occasions. Your talking stick may be a walking stick or any piece of found wood. Decorate it with ribbons and mementoes.

You might like to select the wood for its associations: oak for majesty, hazel for inspiration and wisdom, beech for creativity, ash for prophecy and making connections, apple for love and fertility, willow for intuition, or yew to maintain ancestral links.

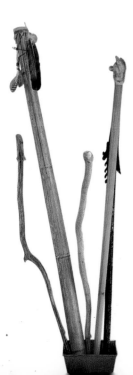

REMOTE CONTROL

Your TV is most unmagical—don't let it take over. Once, the family used the living room to get together and swap stories; now we often congregate to goggle at the box, paying little attention to each other. The focal point should be the fireplace (if you have one), not the screen, so try to ensure the screen does not dominate. If possible, place your television in a cabinet, only opening it for viewing sessions, so that the family can talk, play games, read, and relax. Our TV cannot be placed in a cupboard, so I cover it with an attractive cloth. Keep colorful, interesting books in the living room, maybe even setting your current favorite in a special place, ready for family storytime. Crystals are believed to absorb radiation, and I like to have a sizeable one dangling over the screen. Another idea is to place a glittering geode on top of the appliance. Every so often, cleanse your TV crystal under running water, imagining all the white noise leaving it. Thank your crystal for maintaining a connection with the natural and the timeless, and for clearing the atmosphere of your home.

HAPPY FAMILY HEARTH SPELL

The hearth (in other words, the stove) in the kitchen of the modern home is its working center, but the hearth in the living room is its emotional center. From here, the security and solidity of the home radiate outwards. Here we experience the true delight of being at home. To keep the heart of your home beating strong and true, perform this spell.

You will need a large and beautiful red stone. You may find a stone of a dull red color while out on a walk, but it is worth investing a little money in a semi-precious stone for this focal point. Choose one as large as possible. Non-gem quality rubies signify joy and wealth, garnet bestows strength, carnelian brings peace, healing, and good verbal expression, while red tourmaline gives strength and courage. All these stones are protective. If you wish, you could arrange a group of stones to catch the light, like trapped flames. You will also need a solid earthenware bowl to hold the stone(s), or, if you have one, you could arrange them in the fireplace itself, if you don't use it for a fire, just as many people use this space for a plant.

Take up your red stone and face south, preferably in sunlight. If you are using more than one stone, hold them all if you can do so comfortably, but if not, choose the largest as a "conductor." Feel the warmth of the Sun on you, let it fill you and radiate into the stone you are holding, while you visualize your home filled with warmth and love. Affirm that this is so.

Now take your stone(s) and walk around the outside of your house. If you live in an apartment, you can complete all or part of your circuit indoors. Imagine your home surrounded by warmth. When you've done this, place your stone(s) back in the fireplace in the earthenware bowl and affirm that the protection and blessing of which the stone is the center radiate to the edge of the building, keeping all within safe and warm.

Light a night light within a protective container. This is the sacred flame of your hearth. You could light this whenever the family are all settled in the living room, especially on special occasions and festivals.

Your home has a heart that is strong, true, and warm.

Say It With Flowers

THE FLOWERS APPEAR ON THE EARTH;
THE TIME OF THE SINGING OF BIRDS IS COME,
AND THE VOICE OF THE TURTLE IS HEARD IN OUR LAND

THE BIBLE, Song of Solomon 2:12

Everyone loves flowers, and fresh flowers in a room make it vibrant, sweet, and very special. All flowers are a gift and a celebration, but they have specific meanings and were used to convey messages by many ancient cultures including the Chinese, Egyptians, Greeks, and Indians. Find out what the flowers on your windowsill or dining table mean—for if they were a present, perhaps they carry unconscious significance—and what they are specifically bringing as a gift to your home.

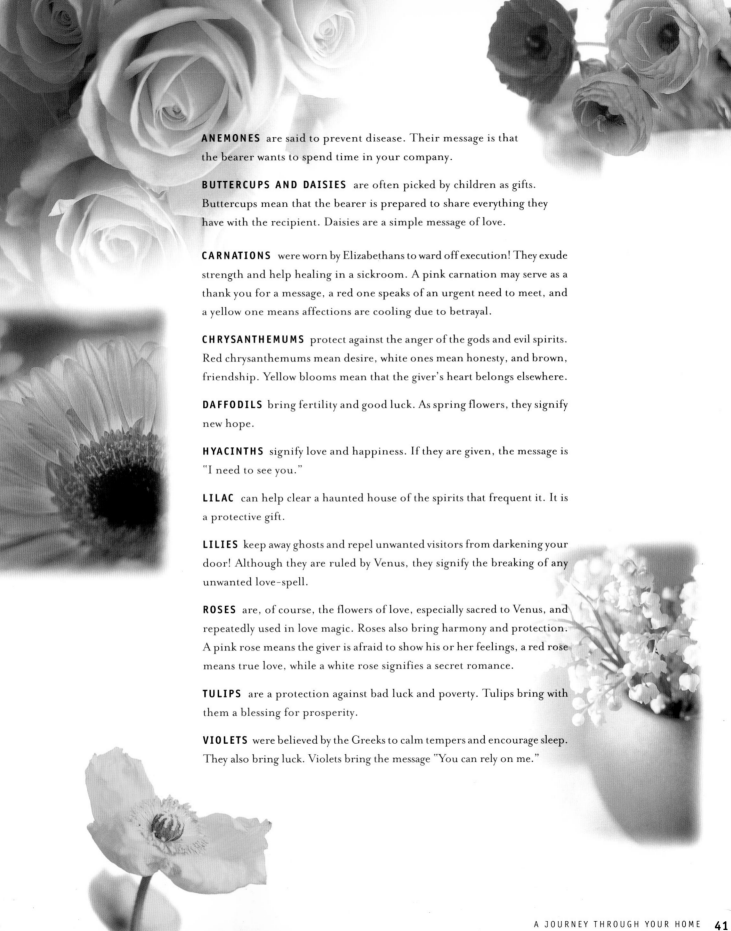

ANEMONES are said to prevent disease. Their message is that the bearer wants to spend time in your company.

BUTTERCUPS AND DAISIES are often picked by children as gifts. Buttercups mean that the bearer is prepared to share everything they have with the recipient. Daisies are a simple message of love.

CARNATIONS were worn by Elizabethans to ward off execution! They exude strength and help healing in a sickroom. A pink carnation may serve as a thank you for a message, a red one speaks of an urgent need to meet, and a yellow one means affections are cooling due to betrayal.

CHRYSANTHEMUMS protect against the anger of the gods and evil spirits. Red chrysanthemums mean desire, white ones mean honesty, and brown, friendship. Yellow blooms mean that the giver's heart belongs elsewhere.

DAFFODILS bring fertility and good luck. As spring flowers, they signify new hope.

HYACINTHS signify love and happiness. If they are given, the message is "I need to see you."

LILAC can help clear a haunted house of the spirits that frequent it. It is a protective gift.

LILIES keep away ghosts and repel unwanted visitors from darkening your door! Although they are ruled by Venus, they signify the breaking of any unwanted love-spell.

ROSES are, of course, the flowers of love, especially sacred to Venus, and repeatedly used in love magic. Roses also bring harmony and protection. A pink rose means the giver is afraid to show his or her feelings, a red rose means true love, while a white rose signifies a secret romance.

TULIPS are a protection against bad luck and poverty. Tulips bring with them a blessing for prosperity.

VIOLETS were believed by the Greeks to calm tempers and encourage sleep. They also bring luck. Violets bring the message "You can rely on me."

TRUE FRIENDSHIP SPELL

One of the greatest blessings in life is to have good friends, and if you can think of at least one person you could phone at 3 a.m. in a crisis, then you are more fortunate than most. Your home will be all the richer if it contains small gifts from friends and if it creates an ambience that attracts and welcomes the people whose friendship you value.

You need a hyacinth bulb or bulbs for this spell. Any color will do, but you could choose pink if you most value warmth and affection, white for truth and faithfulness, and blue if you want calm interaction and discussion.

Take some compost and place it in a wide bowl that will go with your decor. Touch it lovingly, enjoying the richness of the soil on your fingertips—you are creating a place to nurture the closeness and support you need. Now take your hyacinth(s) and plant it or them following the instructions on the package. Imagine yourself creating the beginnings of friendship, sending signals into the earth for the pals you need.

Wait patiently for the first magical green shoots to pierce the top of the soil. Even though little may be happening in your life, know that good influences are growing for you and will soon appear. Meanwhile, keep going out and doing all the day-to-day things that are necessary to meet people and form friendships.

When the shoots appear, place the hyacinth on your windowsill. Place two mugs or glasses next to it; wash or replace them every day. Press several crystals into the soil around the hyacinth and imagine them intensifying the radiance of the plant, sending out welcoming and friendly signals to anyone suitable. You can choose crystals to coordinate with the color of the flower, if you wish. Water your hyacinth carefully and lovingly. As you inhale its scent, imagine and affirm that you are drawing in affection and good company.

When you feel you have established a true and supportive friendship, you will know what to give your friend as a gift—a fragrant hyacinth in a pot!

> Hyacinths grow well indoors and have a wonderful fragrance. They are ruled by Venus and used magically for love and happiness. A hyacinth can be used to draw new friends your way and to strengthen old friendships.

Great Guests

WELCOME IS THE BEST CHEER

Greek proverb

The secret of having great guests is to be a great host or hostess—and the secret of being a great host is to be a genuinely delighted one! Be truly pleased to show off your magical house and have the company of friends.

Good entertaining is more than providing comfort—it is adding a sense of fun so that the conversation flows, everyone laughs, and time flies. The spell on the next page has a star theme, because that shape suggests sparkle and success, and also because stars are time-honored magical symbols.

The five-pointed star signifies the four elements being put to work by the power of the human mind, represented by the fifth apex. It is also sacred to the Goddess because it looks like a female figure. The six-pointed star combines triangles, which also signify the elements. It has been called the Seal of Solomon, and ancient texts describe how Solomon used it to control demons. Any star will dispel the demons of boredom and stagnation from your living room.

THE BEST SEAT IN THE HOUSE

It is a Chinese custom to have an Honored Guest chair. This chair is placed at the far end of the room, facing the door. We all feel most secure and at ease when we have the wall behind us, no one behind our backs, and can see who is coming and going. Obviously, if you have several guests, they cannot all be seated in this way, but do your best, bearing this in mind.

A STELLAR GATHERING

For this spell you will need to make or buy some cinnamon cookies. Cinnamon is ruled by the Sun and brings warmth, success, and love. If you make them yourself, use a star-shaped cookie cutter, and if you buy the cookies, top them with small stars made out of rolled fondant icing, or even paint a star on each cookie with food coloring. Every cookie should carry this symbol. If any guests are on a diet, try cutting apples crosswise to expose the little star at the center. Sprinkle them with lemon juice to prevent them going brown, and add a little heartening cinnamon. Provide other bite-size fruit such as grapes. Continue the star theme into napkins and dishes if you can—hunt down star-shaped plates or ones with star designs. If you bring your cookies in on a tray, decorate the tray with star-shaped table confetti.

Before your guests come, enchant your cookies or fruit. Place them in front of you, holding your hands out toward them with palms downwards. Imagine fun, laughter, and warmth going from your hands into the treats. If you make the cookies yourself, you can do this before they go in the oven. If you like, draw a star in the air over the cookies.

Light a star-shaped candle in your living room and serve coffee in mugs decorated with stars. Whether your guests notice the theme or not, they will catch the vibes. All should be informal and effortless—so much the better if the china isn't all coordinated. Make sure that you are light-hearted and really enjoy having these people in your home.

Your get-together will be heavenly—what a star you are!

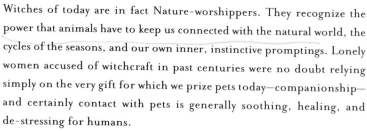

Pet Magic

**WHEN I PLAY WITH MY CAT, WHO KNOWS WHETHER SHE
IS NOT AMUSING HERSELF WITH ME MORE THAN I WITH HER?**

MICHEL DE MONTAIGNE, *Essays II XII*

Witches of today are in fact Nature-worshippers. They recognize the power that animals have to keep us connected with the natural world, the cycles of the seasons, and our own inner, instinctive promptings. Lonely women accused of witchcraft in past centuries were no doubt relying simply on the very gift for which we prize pets today—companionship—and certainly contact with pets is generally soothing, healing, and de-stressing for humans.

If you are an animal lover, don't feel you have to reason away the feelings you have for your pet. Instead, begin to observe your pet closely. Animals have been employed in divination-magic, where Grimalkin's paw selected the tarot card, or rune, that could foretell the future. There are plenty of documented cases of animals who apparently knew what their owners were doing even when they were far from home; watch your cat or dog for signs that they know when a loved one is coming home, are aware of a change in the weather, or the phase of the Moon.

To attune your home deeply and gently to the tides of Nature, be sure to not only love and care for your animals but respect them, too. Follow their wisdom and let their healing influence permeate your dwelling.

PET DETECTIVES

Your pet's choice of sleeping place may give you valuable information. Dogs are said to gravitate toward spots that are healthy for humans, whereas cats are drawn to negative vibrations because they are able—and willing—to neutralize them.

ANCIENT ANIMAL WISDOM

In the old days it was believed that witches had "familiars" —animals that lived with them and with whom they had a magical and sinister connection. Like many myths, this has some basis in fact, for it may be linked to shamanism. This is the art of spirit journeying practiced in many tribal societies. Subtle links were fostered with "totem" animals in order to draw on their power when the shaman was out of his body. In this way, the shaman added to his abilities by contact with the natural world.

SPELL FOR A LOST PET

This spell does not have the power to return to life a pet which has met
with an accident, but it should bring you news sooner rather than later.

Take a length of twine long enough to stretch from your window or door
onto the ground outside. Attach to it something belonging to your pet—
a toy, special mat, or maybe just some shed hairs. Alternatively, write your pet's
name on a piece of paper, roll this up, and attach it to the end of the twine.

Dangle your twine outside and call your pet. Now, slowly and steadily,
draw the length of twine in toward you. As you do so, imagine your pet
returning, hear the sound of its paws, smell its fur, hear its bark or purr.
Concentrate on this for as long as you are able.

Roll up your twine and special object and keep them where your pet
usually sleeps. Repeat this on subsequent days until your pet returns or
you hear news. Hopefully you will soon have some good tidings!

Precious Privacy

Wanting to be by ourselves may be something of
which we feel a little ashamed—as if it is not quite
healthy to be solitary. But being alone can be
a great source of peace. In addition, sometimes it
is necessary to be alone, to think, work, or complete
a project. You may even want to avoid a specific person
or group of people. At times like these, we all need a little
help from hidden forces, to protect our privacy and the
sanctity of our home. Of course, closing the curtains,
taking the phone off the hook, and playing soft music will
work wonders, and a magical house that is psychically
protected will offer better
shelter than most. But for
those times when more is
needed, here is a spell.

YOUR INVISIBLE CIRCLE

You will need a dark blue candle, an oil burner, some dill, and oil of myrrh.
Sit quietly in the place where you most want to be alone, and rub the myrrh
oil onto the candle, thinking as you do so of all the places where you have
been peacefully solitary, perhaps on a deserted beach or in woodland. Place
the candle in a holder and sprinkle the dill around it. Say:

Be encircled by protection, be encircled by invisibility, be encircled by silence.

Take the dill and go around the outside of your dwelling, repeating the
affirmation as you do so. Imagine you are sealing yourself off from the
outside world. Imagine there is a protective bubble around your house
and that all who approach it simply lose interest and turn away.

Go back inside and mentally affirm to yourself, as you close the door,
that you are shutting out unwanted intrusions. Place an offering of dill
before the god or goddess figure on your altar, asking them for protection.

Return to your candle. Light it and heat the oil in the burner. Imagine
the protective bubble becoming a shell enclosing you and your home, so
that even the noise of passing traffic sounds muffled, as if by snow.

Now get on with your project—or your relaxation.

Dismantle your protection when you want to interact again. Mentally
reabsorb your bubble, and clear up as much of the dill as you can. Light
a yellow candle, and imagine the radiance spreading out and illuminating
your home. Get ready for all those thwarted callers to catch up with you!

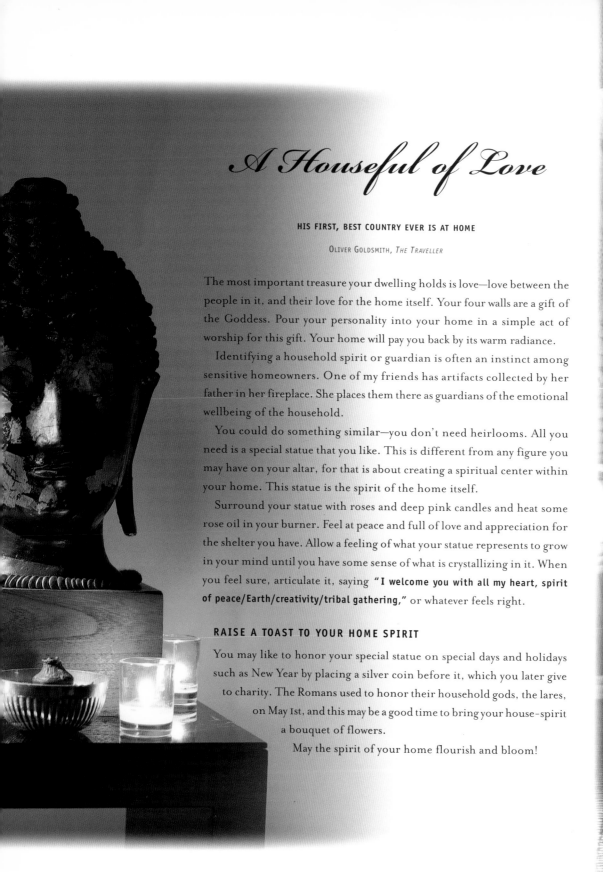

A Houseful of Love

HIS FIRST, BEST COUNTRY EVER IS AT HOME

Oliver Goldsmith, *The Traveller*

The most important treasure your dwelling holds is love—love between the people in it, and their love for the home itself. Your four walls are a gift of the Goddess. Pour your personality into your home in a simple act of worship for this gift. Your home will pay you back by its warm radiance.

Identifying a household spirit or guardian is often an instinct among sensitive homeowners. One of my friends has artifacts collected by her father in her fireplace. She places them there as guardians of the emotional wellbeing of the household.

You could do something similar—you don't need heirlooms. All you need is a special statue that you like. This is different from any figure you may have on your altar, for that is about creating a spiritual center within your home. This statue is the spirit of the home itself.

Surround your statue with roses and deep pink candles and heat some rose oil in your burner. Feel at peace and full of love and appreciation for the shelter you have. Allow a feeling of what your statue represents to grow in your mind until you have some sense of what is crystallizing in it. When you feel sure, articulate it, saying **"I welcome you with all my heart, spirit of peace/Earth/creativity/tribal gathering,"** or whatever feels right.

RAISE A TOAST TO YOUR HOME SPIRIT

You may like to honor your special statue on special days and holidays such as New Year by placing a silver coin before it, which you later give to charity. The Romans used to honor their household gods, the lares, on May 1st, and this may be a good time to bring your house-spirit a bouquet of flowers.

May the spirit of your home flourish and bloom!

YOUR HOME SPIRIT

A friend of mine moved into a two-hundred-year-old cottage and became aware of the strong atmosphere already present. Although she loved the house, she felt the need to put her own stamp upon it, and also to make contact with the spirit of the place. She decided to honor her home by commissioning a sculptor to make a special statue. When the beautiful thing arrived it held a sense of movement, and so she decided that it was a wind spirit—just what the old house needed to bring in a breath of fresh life. She asked me to consecrate the statue, which we did at a small party, asking especially for the spirits of Air to infuse the sculpture and protect the home.

The Energy Center

The kitchen is the true center of your home. It is the warmest and often the chattiest place, as folk seem to gravitate toward the source of their sustenance! Your kitchen should be much more than utilitarian, for it is the energy center and origin of life's "feel-good factor." Have some items on display in the kitchen. This is an action room, so tools should double as ornaments—chunky saucepans, earthenware jars, spices, fruit and vegetables, and colorful mugs all serve as culinary inspiration.

FOCUS ON YOUR FRIDGE

Make your fridge a magical focus in the kitchen by transforming its bare surface with a symbolic display of magnets. Think creatively. What does your kitchen require? Need some help thinking clearly at the end of the day? Extend your dinnertime inventiveness by bird-shaped magnets—or even a winged head, such as I have on my fridge. Happiness and welcome can be created by suns, hearts, and smiling faces. Extra nourishment may be conjured by ears of wheat and fruit-shaped magnets, connection with your family through magnetic photo frames, cozy familiarity by dogs and cats—the list is limited only by your imagination.

You can also create a complete "ritual center" on your fridge by depicting the four elements, Earth, Air, Fire, and Water, and using them for impromptu spells. Need extra support and understanding? Clip a daisy or a sprig of herbs under your Water symbol. Wanting more prosperity? Hang a gold necklace from your Earth symbol. You can be as inventive as you like, regrouping your magnets whenever you wish, to generate a new phase for the family. See page 126 for more ideas.

KITCHEN HEARTH GODDESS

Vesta was the Roman goddess of the hearth and food preparation. A sacred flame was kept burning eternally in her worship, and maidens from noble families came to serve her in Rome as the Vestal Virgins. Her fire symbolizes and nurtures the fire of life. You might like to choose a suitable figurine to keep next to your stove or on your windowsill to remind you of the sacred aspect of cooking, where we use the gifts of the Earth to nourish us. On special occasions, place a little of the meal before Vesta and afterwards, place it outside for animals, birds, or simply as an offering to the Earth. Vesta was especially honored on February 13th, at the Full Moon at the beginning of May, and on June 7th, and at these times you may like to place a small bouquet in front of her, or leave her in moonlight or sunlight, so she may bless your kitchen all the more.

May the fires of your kitchen burn heartily!

Using the Element of Fire

NOW STIR THE FIRE, AND CLOSE THE SHUTTERS FAST
LET FALL THE CURTAINS, WHEEL THE SOFA ROUND

WILLIAM COWPER, *THE WINTER EVENING*

Fire is a transforming element, much revered by the ancients. Traditionally it has been used in many ways, from changing the shape of metals to heating our homes and making our food. Fire is inspiration, warmth, creativity—and sadly, it is lacking in many modern homes.

From having pride of place in the hearth, Fire has now largely disappeared from our lives. Instead of leaping flames, we have radiators and microwaves. However, in our hearts we miss the Fire, the showering sparks, the dancing shadows, the enchanted pictures we could have seen as we looked into the molten cavern in the grate.

The kitchen is the true home of Fire, and with a little effort you can invite the element back in to yours. Consider substituting a gas stove for electric, and feel your spirits leap with its immediate heat. Keep use of the microwave to a minimum. Its inward heating system does not fittingly represent the element of Fire, so it won't bring any magic into your kitchen. Best of all, install a wood-fired stove, for a real glow.

Candles are popular because they are one of the few sources of true Fire. Keep plenty in your kitchen, perhaps lighting one on the windowsill or next to a figure of Vesta, goddess of the hearth, to signal the start of meal preparation. Wood, as well as being a rich, hearty material, has an affinity with Fire. In times gone by, people believed that Fire dwelt within wood, waiting to be kindled. The Chinese elemental system has a cycle in which Wood generates Fire. So add wooden dishes, cutting boards, and cupboard doors to your kitchen. Sunflowers, allspice, rosemary, bay, basil, cinnamon, cumin, garlic, onion, mustard, pepper, orange, and tea are all traditionally linked to Fire, so display these for a fiery ambience.

Come in out of the cold—to the welcome of Fire in your kitchen!

Herbs for Medicine and Magic

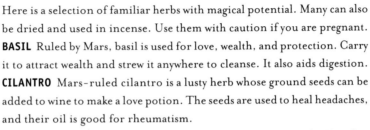

Here is a selection of familiar herbs with magical potential. Many can also be dried and used in incense. Use them with caution if you are pregnant.

BASIL Ruled by Mars, basil is used for love, wealth, and protection. Carry it to attract wealth and strew it anywhere to cleanse. It also aids digestion.

CILANTRO Mars-ruled cilantro is a lusty herb whose ground seeds can be added to wine to make a love potion. The seeds are used to heal headaches, and their oil is good for rheumatism.

DILL Mercury rules dill, which is used in money and love spells. Placed in their cribs it protects little ones. Sniff dill to stop hiccups.

MARJORAM Mercury rules this herb. It brings love, health, and happiness.

MINT Ruled by Venus (though some say Mercury), mint is used magically for protection, money, lust, healing, travel, and cleansing. Place mint on your altar—as I do frequently—to draw good influences into your life.

PARSLEY Ruled by Mercury, parsley protects, purifies, and arouses lust. Tradition states it will only grow for the head of the household. It sweetens the breath, especially after eating garlic, and aids digestion.

ROSEMARY Ruled by the Sun, rosemary can be used as a substitute for frankincense in incense. It is purifying, positive, and healing. Place it under your pillow for a good sleep and no nightmares. It soothes digestion and aids memory. Rosemary may swiftly outgrow a windowsill.

SAGE Ruled by Jupiter, this herb is lucky, bestowing longevity, wealth, and protection. Carry sage to be wise. It has antiseptic properties and may help offset the toxicity in pork. An infusion helps sore throats and ulcers.

THYME This is ruled by Venus. Thyme gives psychic gifts, courage, love, health, and sleep, and is good for flatulence, coughs, and diarrhea.

Nourished in Every Way

In your dining room, more is—or should be—taken in than just food. As we eat, we become part of the cycle of existence. All life depends on death, for everything we swallow was once a living plant or being. While this may not be an appetizing thought, we still honor the sacrificial nature of eating by making meals an occasion. Your dining room may be about three things—simple enjoyment, social exchange, and a hint of the sacred.

Shades of orange, apricot, cream, and peach are stimulating to the appetite, so if possible, choose them for dining decor. If you do not have a separate dining room, feature these colors in an alcove or use them in tablecloths, napkins, and centerpieces. Try to keep your dining area free of distractions such as books and magazines. Even if you are eating alone, make the basic business of eating pleasurable by itself, even if only for a few minutes—you will be more likely to do this if you have a pretty table centerpiece or pleasant view to attract your gaze.

THE GREEN MAN

Whatever your religious beliefs, saying grace is a pleasant idea, because it acknowledges we are part of a greater process. A simple "Thank you for giving your lives to feed us" and the lighting of a candle make an occasion of a meal. Our dining room features a picture of the Green Man, spirit of vegetation, and representation of the ever-renewing process of life. The Green Man is carved in many churches and may have been Medieval masons' salute to secret pagan beliefs. He (sometimes she) is a foliate mask, a face made of leaves, sometimes appearing to "speak" the leaves. The Green Man has many meanings, from the simple—all life is sentient—to more subtle matters, such as true eloquence comes from harmony with Nature. You may wish to honor this idea by wreathing an apricot candle with some ivy and evergreen fronds, and lighting it as your meal commences.

FEED THE SPIRIT

Nourish yourself mentally by featuring achievements, such as trophies and certificates, in your dining room. In our dining room the children's paintings are displayed and the family noticeboard prompts mealtime conversation. One of my friends has a streamer of cards that have been sent to the family, permanently on display. This is a reminder of happy times. It is important to laugh and feel good while you eat.

Using the Element of Earth

WHILE THE EARTH REMAINETH, SEEDTIME AND HARVEST, AND COLD AND HEAT, AND
SUMMER AND WINTER, AND DAY AND NIGHT SHALL NOT CEASE

The Bible, Genesis 8:22

Earth is associated with all that is stable, enduring, nourishing, protecting, and grounding. It is the "touchy-feely" element of the senses. It is given pride of place by modern pagans, who place the altar for their rituals to the north, which is the quarter associated with Earth. In the north of the sky, Sun and Moon do not roam, so it is the home of the mysterious and the dark, the tomb that is also the womb. (These positions are reversed in the southern hemisphere.) Life comes from the earth and returns to the earth, in order to be born again.

Because Earth nourishes us and provides the food we eat, the dining room is the appropriate place to honor it. Choose pictures for this room that are a reminder of the natural cycle, such as wheat fields or Constable prints. Continue the theme with coasters and tablemats showing country scenes, animals, and greenery. Luxuriant plants are especially appropriate in the dining area, for they are a testament to your respect for Earth as well as your use of it. If you have room, a slab of smooth stone, preferably local to the area in which you live, may be placed at the center of the table to receive hot dishes and candlesticks.

Instead of growing parsley in your kitchen, consider giving this brilliant green herb a place in your dining room. It is ruled by the planet Mercury (which rules the Earth sign Virgo, sign of the harvest), and Mercury was the only god who could travel in and out of the Underworld with impunity. Parsley has links with the Underworld, but also with protection, and it has the function of guarding food from contamination. Honor the Earth by garnishing special dishes with this plant, to show respect for the natural cycle. This may be a mini-ritual before special meals. Nip off the sprigs with your fingernail, don't cut them—and remember to thank the plant.

Dowsing Your Food

For the first time in history, people in the developed world have an endless supply of all types of food. Enough food is no longer a problem, but eating the right food is more and more so, for modern food additives, plus the dangers of obesity, mean we need to consider carefully what we eat.

On pages 14–15 we encountered dowsing to evaluate food. If you or your family have allergies, digestive problems, or similar, you may like to make this a priority. Select a crystal especially for food dowsing and keep it in a soft pouch of green or brown cloth in a safe place in your kitchen. Keep with it small cards on which you have written the names of each person you have to feed. Whenever you are uncertain about a food or additive, hold the pendulum over it and keep the forefinger of your non-dowsing hand on the name of the person concerned. Ask the pendulum **"Is this food suitable for...?"** and watch for your yes/no swing.

As you become more practiced, a picture of the food or a written recipe can replace the actual food, on which you may not want to waste your money. You may like to have dowsing sessions where you try several foods with your pendulum and then record the results. The pendulum can also tell you what to eat if you are off-color, want to boost your vitality, or generally build up or cut down. Just ask a clear question, such as **"Will this food help with...?"** Remember that a swing from side to side means "maybe." Dowsing food can also be useful for dinner parties—if you are not sure what to give a tricky guest, get some secret help in the kitchen.

Get in the swing and be the cook, host, or hostess with the mostest.

Magical Meals

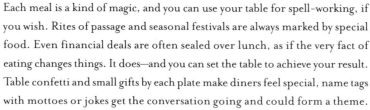

HE WHO DOES NOT MIND HIS BELLY, WILL HARDLY MIND ANYTHING ELSE

Samuel Johnson

Each meal is a kind of magic, and you can use your table for spell-working, if you wish. Rites of passage and seasonal festivals are always marked by special food. Even financial deals are often sealed over lunch, as if the very fact of eating changes things. It does—and you can set the table to achieve your result. Table confetti and small gifts by each plate make diners feel special, name tags with mottoes or jokes get the conversation going and could form a theme.

A beautifully laid table is a rite in itself—you won't be wasting time on something that will only last a short while, because it will make a difference to all who partake. Do you want prosperity for the family? Lay your table with a gold cloth and purple napkins, bringing in the colors of the Sun and Jupiter, and choose candles to coordinate. Include sage, cloves, maple syrup, or chestnuts in the menu for Jupiter; rosemary, sunflower seeds, cinnamon, or oranges for the Sun. As you all sit down, say **"This meal marks the beginning of a successful, prosperous period—let us celebrate in advance."** Make sure the conversation is cheerful and positive. As another example, a meal to create harmony could start with a table laid in pale pink and blue, and include Venus substances such as apple, apricot, avocado, thyme, tomato, or peach. See the table on page 126 for more. Be inventive!

You could have a meal to celebrate Full Moon, with the table laid with silver and a large white or silver candle in the center. Dishes could include white food such as chicken, fish, bananas, and white chocolate. Such a meal provides an opportunity for the family to talk about their creativity. Seasonal meals for Christmas, May Eve, and Halloween may have the same magic ingredients year after year.

It is traditional at Halloween to use food for divination, baking symbols (such as a key, a coin, or a button) in a pudding and so, telling the fortune of the person in whose portion they appear. Coins in pudding at Christmas are similar. You might like to shuffle a pack of divinatory cards and place one under each person's tablemat. Of course, for family meals all predictions should be favorable, so suggesting to each person that they are filling up with good fortune. Eat your way to enchantment!

SEASONAL CENTERPIECE

A friend of mine has as her permanent centerpiece a very large breakfast cup and saucer given to her grandmother as a wedding present. The saucer she fills with seasonal edibles such as nuts and fruits, the cup with inedibles such as flowers, acorns, and leaves. To complete the arrangement, a candle of an appropriate color goes in the cup. You might like to adapt this idea for yourself— you do not need to have an heirloom to start a tradition!

Using the Element of Air

MAKE THE BABBLING GOSSIP OF THE AIR
CRY OUT

WILLIAM SHAKESPEARE, *TWELFTH NIGHT*

Air is the element associated by occultists with the power of thought, communication, study, chatter, and journeys. Light, bright, mobile, impossible to catch but powerful enough to bend mighty branches, Air is fresh and free, touching all, contained by nothing. Whatever occupation you follow, this element has its proper home in your study or work area, bringing you ideas and keeping your mind open and adaptable.

You can invite Air into your study the easy way, by opening a window, and this you should do every day, even if only for a minute. Trees are especially associated with Air, and you are certainly blessed if you can see them from your study window. If not, you might like to have a wooden wand or artifacts on your desk to play with while you are seeking inspiration. Hazel is a good choice as it is associated with wisdom and insight (see page 37 for the special properties of other woods).

Specific gifts of Air enwrap you when you use essential oils and incense. Lavender is ruled by the planet Mercury, and Mercury rules the most sparkly, chatty, vivacious Air sign of them all—Gemini. Choose an attractive receptacle for your lavender incense or oil, and make a small ritual of lighting it as you prepare to apply yourself. After a while, this will have the effect of getting you in the right frame of mind. Any scent you like will work well, but don't just choose smells because they are "nice"—be aware of the effect any scent has on you, because in your study you want something to help you think and create.

Take a deep breath—and get to work!

Wonderful Work

Concentration is less discipline, more inspiration. If you are motivated to work, what you produce will be better by far than anything ground out through gritted teeth! So nothing in your study should distract you. It is not a place to dump shopping or store household items waiting to be fixed. Clear it at the end of each day, so when you next come in, you can start right away. Make your work area attractive—a vase of flowers on the desk or a cheerful pot to hold pens tells you that work is pleasant.

EXPRESS YOURSELF

If you work from home, your study is probably more than the place where you earn your daily bread—it is an expression of you. Make the first thing you see as you go in to work something that spells achievement. If you are a painter, your best-ever painting, elegantly framed, should have pride of place; if you are an accountant, feature your qualifications and letters of appreciation. Wreathe fresh bay leaves around your achievements, for bay (*Laurus nobilis*) represents your laurels.

MOTIVATE YOURSELF

Seats of learning have had mottoes since ancient times. For instance, in the temple at Delphi in ancient Greece was the inscription "Know Thyself." Think of a motto or slogan that is special to you. My work as a writer on magic can lay me open to criticism, so over my desk I have the words "A wolf that does not howl will never find her pack," with a picture of a wolf's head (my birth totem in some Native American traditions). All this is special to me, and encouraging as I sit down to work. You, too, need a key phrase to speed you on your creative path. Find it, and frame it!

Color Me Creative

THE PUREST AND MOST THOUGHTFUL MINDS ARE THOSE WHICH LOVE COLOR THE MOST

JOHN RUSKIN, *THE STONES OF VENICE*

Different colors have different effects on the mind. You will naturally sense these effects, but planetary links with various colors clarify their "vibrational" qualities (for more color links, see page 126). Blue and yellow makes a serene yet stimulating scheme for your study, a room in which you need to achieve.

SHADES FOR YOUR STUDY

COLOR	PLANET	EFFECT/VIBRATION
Blue	VENUS	Calm, peaceful, and healing
Purple-blue	JUPITER	Opulence
Deep blue	SATURN	Concentration
Electric blue	URANUS	Excitement
Yellow	MERCURY	Energy, transformation

Blue, the color of the sky, has a cooling, liberating effect, while yellow energizes without overpowering— it is transformative, vitalizing mental powers and encouraging wisdom. Look at covering curtains, carpets, and walls in these colors, and continue the theme into accessories. Place a blue candle in a golden holder, yellow potpourri in a blue bowl, decorate a blue tub for pens and brushes with gold stars.

You might like to collect some blue and gold throws. When you need the quality of a specific shade, wrap yourself in it. If you can't get down to work, a navy blue wrap around your shoulders may concentrate you; for calm, choose a lighter blue, or yellow for a creative burst. Coordinating candles will also help.

ASK THOTH

A small figurine of the Egyptian god of wisdom, Thoth, carved in blue stone and with a piece of lapis lazuli placed before him, will bring a devotional element to your study. If you need specific help with a project, write your question on yellow paper, roll it into a scroll, and tie it with blue ribbon. Place the scroll in front of Thoth and sleep on the matter!

WORKING WONDERS SPELL

Where does inspiration come from? One thing is sure—when you need it, it is often most elusive! Inspiration cannot be achieved by discipline, hard work, and concentration alone. It needs a subtle magical something to free all those wonderful ideas that lie in your subconscious.

Perform this little spell when you are feeling relaxed and playful, so you are full of potential ideas to store up for use when you need inspiration. You will need a blue pitcher (preferably glass), a blue bottle with a stopper, some spring water, and a crystal to hang in your window.

So much the better if your study faces towards the Sun, but you can do this spell anywhere in your house. Just hang your crystal where it catches the Sun's rays and watch for the little rainbows that it casts around the room—children love to find them. Pour the spring water into your blue pitcher. Catch the rainbow in the water, if you can, or simply let the rainbow fall onto the glass. Look into the pure water and imagine all the rainbow hues within it. Then pour the water into your blue bottle, insert the stopper, and place your bottle somewhere prominent in your study—after all, it coordinates with the color scheme!

Renew this spell every few weeks, so the water stays fresh. Take a swig whenever you need extra inspiration. You have creativity on tap.

MAKING MONEY SPELL

Our culture is often obsessed with money and the status it bestows, and we may have the feeling that it is not quite "nice" to want more money. After all, the best things in life are free—but are they? Money buys the best food and healthcare, education, and travel, and even plays a part in love, for if you cannot afford to look your best you feel less lovable, and if you have no money for socializing, you stand less chance of meeting a lover! Don't feel guilty if you wish for money, for the world has enough riches for all. Take your share and give back where you can.

If you work from home, your study is your money-making center, so it is the best place for some subtle cash conjuring. For this spell, you will need two green candles, some green paper, a pen, some patchouli oil, and a fireproof bowl or pot with a lid. This pot should coordinate with your study and double as an ornament.

When casting money spells, you are limited only by your imagination, but in reality they work better if you believe in the sum. In other words, you can imagine yourself receiving fifty pounds, but fifty thousand might stretch your belief. It is important that the sum seems reasonable to you. Your spell should be for a specific amount of money and, if possible, for a specific purpose. The money may not come simply as a windfall; it may come as an opportunity to earn more, or from several different sources.

Light your candles and relax. Imagine the money coming to you and exactly what you will do with it—how good it is going to feel to have this money, this power to act. When you are ready, write the amount you want on the green paper—perhaps write yourself a mock check. Place a little patchouli oil on the paper, twist it, and set it alight in the candle flame, holding it over the pot until it is all ash (you may need tongs for this).

Replace the lid on the pot and, holding it carefully, take it outside and cast the feathery ash to the winds, making sure none blows back inside.

When your money comes, give a little to charity and burn incense or an incense stick in your magic pot. Spend with wisdom and pleasure!

Peace and Pleasure

Peace is a precious gift in our hectic world. Make your bedroom into a sanctuary of the restful and serene, where you can slip out of the rat race into a soft, new dimension. But remember that peace depends on your state of mind as much as your material surroundings, and it may mean different things to different people.

OUTER PEACE

Begin by creating physical peace. Choose natural colors or muted blues, greens, and lilacs for walls and bedcovers, brightening them with rose, apricot, and burgundy, if necessary. Follow Chinese wisdom and create a minimalist style by making sure there is very little in the bedroom to distract you from sleep. Clothes, books, and any reminders of working life should be firmly behind cupboard doors, and lighting should be soft and set low. Beware of any sharp corners, especially those that point towards the bed, for these may create harmful influences. No mirror should reflect you while you are in bed, and if you must have a TV in the bedroom, make sure it can be covered. Luminous stars on the ceiling and small plaques or pictures showing the Moon and stars give a sleepy vibe. Candles, a CD player, and lavender scent complete the picture.

INNER PEACE

For mental calm, you will need to ask yourself what peace means to you. Peace is not completely synonymous with pleasure, for that may involve excitement, which you wish to avoid. Think what you can add to your bedroom to promote inner peace. A poster of your last holiday

destination might evoke the relaxation you experienced then, perhaps
pictures of loved ones, something you find especially beautiful such as
a jewel (an amethyst geode would be a perfect choice), or even symbols of
your achievements, such as certificates or trophies—only if you like to rest
on your laurels as opposed to being distracted by them, of course!

SWEET DREAMS SPELL

For a little restful help from the subtle realms, enchant a large, cuddly cup or mug in which to make a special drink whenever you wish to unwind. Choose a mug in a shade of blue, purple, or green, to coordinate with your room—all the better if it has moons and stars on it—and make sure it feels good to hold. After the Sun has gone down, light one lavender or blue candle and anoint yourself on the forehead, between your eyes, with a drop of lavender oil. After carefully washing your mug and drying it thoroughly on a fresh cloth, make yourself an herbal tea of your choice, such as chamomile, and sweeten to taste with honey. Place your mug in front of the candle and watch the steam curling upwards. Imagine that your body and your spirit are as light as the steam, breathe in its vapor and feel yourself filled with relaxation. Run your finger clockwise around the rim of the mug, saying three times:

This mug always and ever shall be
A vessel of perfect peace for me.

Put your feet up and sip. Aaah!

Pleasure Dome

PLEASURE'S A SIN, AND SOMETIMES SIN'S A PLEASURE

Lord Byron, *Don Juan*

Turning your bedroom into a pleasure zone will keep your relationship hot and show your lover how much you value the sensual things you share. It will help you turn off from stress and distraction and turn on to love-making. But remember that the mind also is an erogenous zone and that subtlety often works best.

SETTING THE SCENE

Your bed will be your den of delight, so buy the largest, best-quality one you can, and make sure everything on and close to it is sumptuous. Choose rugs for tactile appeal as well as appearance, and walk on carpets barefoot before you buy them to test for softness. If you fancy black satin sheets, try to test the fabric against bare skin. It may be too cold (and cosy cotton more sensuous) when you are naked. Warm colors such as pinks, deep reds, and black create a "sinful" ambience.

Have everything you need close by. On your bedside table, place a bowl of fruit, twin goblets in rose-tinted glass, wine, a water jug, and a heart-shaped box of chocolates. Piles of sinky cushions should be there, to arrange to suit you both. Massage oils in attractive bottles, plush towels that coordinate with the bedding, scents, candles, and music are all part of your bedside checklist.

GIFT OF THE GODS

Remember that all love-making is an energy-exchange and, in a sense, a sacrament. Make room on a cupboard top for a god and goddess figure or a sculpture of an embracing couple. A yin and yang design might serve the same purpose. On special occasions, burn oil of ylang-ylang, rose, or jasmine, bring a fresh red rose or sprig of thyme as an offering and burn two deep red candles. Consecrate rings, other jewelry, or special clothes by leaving them next to your sacred figures while you make love, for passion is a gift of the gods.

LOVERS' CHARM

Why not make a special chaplet as a love-charm to place around a lampshade or hang on a bedpost? Twist a stalk of rosemary into a circle and secure it with a little wire or green thread. Weave a red ribbon around it or, if you wish, a red and a blue ribbon for male and female (or any other two colors that seem appropriate). Weave a hair from each of your heads into the chaplet. You can include silk flowers, too—avoid dried ones, for they are unlucky. Consecrate your lovers' charm by linking hands through it.

SWEET HARMONY SPELL

We all know relationships need working at, but this work is really a pleasure. We can use simple rituals and lovely objects in the home to remind ourselves of what is really important. Whenever things are becoming fraught, bring harmony back with this spell.

You will need an attractive, large crystal or glass bowl, a quart or two of spring water, a large white candle, and some ylang-ylang or jasmine oil. When the Moon is full, fill the bowl with spring water, light the candle, and place the bowl where the moonlight can fall upon it. Let two drops of oil fall into the water. After washing your hands, you and your lover should immerse your fingers in the moonlit water and link them. Talk of the pleasant sensations you feel, or keep silent. Touch each other's faces and lips if you wish, and smile.

If your lover doesn't want to take part in the spell, omit the oil and just dip your fingers into the water while imagining love and harmony between you. Then use a little of the water to make your partner a hot drink! However, be sure your partner really wants the same things as you, for no spell should influence the life path of another against his or her wishes.

This spell can be done using candlelight if there is no Moon visible. Leave your beautiful bowl of harmony where you can see it as you walk into the bedroom. Place floating candles and blossoms in it to keep the atmosphere serene at all times.

DELIGHTFUL DREAMS

We all dream every night, whether we remember it or not, and in this way we work through our daily conflicts and refresh our minds for the morning. To ensure your dreams are sweet and pleasant, hang a dream-catcher over your bed.

In Native American tradition, the dream-catcher snares bad dreams that come floating near you and lets through the good ones. You can make your own dream-catcher by bending a willow twig into a loop and winding fabric tape around it. Next, sew lengths of thick cotton thread or strands of cord at right angles across it, forming a web. Within that web, place your own symbols, beads, or other objects. The one over our bed has a minute figure of a bear for protection and an arrowhead for dreams that travel swiftly, far beyond the day-to-day world. Below it hang two feathers, which are further symbols of flight.

Alternatively, you can buy a dream-catcher in a New Age shop and make it special to you by anointing it with some of your favorite essential oil, interweaving some of your hair in its strands, or attaching your own special silver charm or symbol such as a heart or a key.

Vary your dream-catcher to attract the dreams you want, for example a sprig of fresh lavender for peace and clarity, jasmine for prophecy, mint or rosemary for lust. See page 126 for more ideas. Dream on!

The Bewitched Wardrobe

**FINE CLOTHES, RICH FURNITURE, JEWELS, AND PLATE
ARE MORE INVITING THAN BEAUTY UNADORNED**

Aphra Behn, *The Rover*

Your wardrobe is your den of witchery, from which you conjure a little glamour, rustle up some style, or slip into comfort and relaxation. It all starts here.

Your closet should smell heavenly—not of stale perfume, but of fresh aromas chosen to cherish your clothes. Use herbal sachets to keep away moths and other insects. Fill small muslin bags with dried rosemary, sage, mint, and thyme, and tie them on hangers with ribbon or lace. Lemon is associated both with love and cleanliness, so a lemon pomander is a perfect gift to your cupboard. Stick cloves into the skin of a firm lemon, roll it in mixed spice, wrap it in tissue, and let it dry for several weeks in a warm place before hanging it in your closet. Mmmm!

CLOSET GODDESS

Freya, Norse goddess of beauty, spring, and fertility, was known for her love of adornment. Invoke her blessing by using emblems sacred to her. Place dried rose petals in the bottom of your wardrobe and adorn the outside

with swans, cats, pearls, and silver lunar ornaments.
Say a prayer for beauty to Freya on her day, Friday.
Burn a rose or sandalwood incense stick and waft
it around your closet while you make your request.

Your wardrobe is a metaphor for your secret
self. Sort it regularly, so when you open it to select
clothes, you have a choice, not a battle with mess.
And forget the "expensive mistake." Let it give
pleasure to someone it suits and make room
for something better for you.

Your revitalized closet will inspire you.
You'll never again say you've got
nothing to wear!

BEAUTIFUL YOU

Beauty is in the eye of the beholder, goes the saying. But a wise man also said, "Beauty is in the eye of the beheld." If you believe you are beautiful, most people will find you so. Enchant your mirror, so you see the best in yourself—and make the best of yourself.

The Greek goddess of love and beauty, Aphrodite, was never seen without her mirror. Find an item you associate with Aphrodite, and keep it close for this spell. You will need powdered incense or incense sticks containing rose, and some rose-colored candles. Find a large white or pastel veil and a garland of flowers, preferably roses, to hang over your mirror.

Bathe before you begin and put on your favorite perfume and body lotion. Wear an attractive robe, or go naked. Sip your favorite wine as you sit before the veiled mirror, with candles burning around you, and the fragrance of roses in the air. Describe to yourself all the good qualities about you and your looks. Think of yourself as a lover would, admiring, seeing the best, most fascinating, and individual in every feature. How blessed you are!

When you feel ready, take a candle and walk clockwise three times around the mirror, saying:

Mirror, when I look in thee
Show me the best me I can be.

Stand in front of the mirror, slowly remove the veil and flowers and raise a toast to the beauty that is you. Give thanks to Aphrodite and stroke a little wine round the edge of the mirror.

See yourself as the Goddess made you—gorgeous!

FERTILITY SPELL

Does your home long for the patter of tiny feet? Then it is most likely that the secret and magical beginnings of this new life will start in your bedroom. Try this spell to give Nature a nudge.

This is an ongoing spell that may take a few months, so set aside a little space in your home for it. You will need a green cloth, a small oval bowl (or egg-shaped box, for example from an Easter egg), some ears of wheat (you can find these dried and painted in craft shops) or brown rice, a moonstone, a small goddess figure, two green candles and one white, a stone for each of the phases of the Moon (black for Dark Moon, white for Full Moon, pink for waxing Moon, blue for waning), and some sunflower seeds. You should also have a small piece of topaz, amber, or gold jewelry, a tiny bowl, and a feather.

Spread the green cloth in the place you have chosen and place the oval bowl or half-egg in the center. Make a nest in this with the wheat or brown rice and in it place the moonstone. Stand the goddess figure behind the oval bowl or half-egg. Beside her, place the two green candles with the white one between them. Arrange the Moon-phase stones in front of the white candle. Charge up the topaz, amber, or gold by leaving it in noon sunlight for a few minutes and obtain a little fresh rainwater for the small bowl. Arrange these and the feather on your green cloth as well.

When you feel you are coming to your fertile time of the month, circle the stone that represents the current Moon phase with sunflower seeds. Light the candles and touch the piece of jewelry, feather, and rainwater, linking yourself with the cycles of Nature in sun, wind, and rain. Hold the moonstone against your belly, feeling the light from the white candle entering your womb and growing there like a tiny jewel. Ask the goddess to bless you with a child and imagine what it will be like to be pregnant, give birth, have your own little one. Replace the moonstone carefully in its nest and eat the sunflower seeds.

While you are wishing to become pregnant, get as much fresh air as you can, letting the Sun fall on your face, tasting the rain, and feeling the wind in your hair. Renew or refresh their symbols once a month, preferably at New Moon. Repeat the little ritual whenever you believe you are fertile, but remember that the ways of Nature are mysterious and you may become pregnant at other times, too. Be patient. Soon your nest will be full.

Nurturing Nursery

There is no magic to equal the birth of a perfect, new human. Tiny babies seem very close to Otherworld, as if they were in touch with the whispering of angels—and perhaps they are. Some babies look upon the world with deep and knowing eyes and could be termed "old souls," for they may have had many incarnations upon Earth. Our dearest wish is for our little ones to be healthy and normal. But our task as parents is also to give room for their spirits to grow. A well-thought-out nursery enables them to recall other worlds while they take their place in this one.

Soft colors are nursery favorites, because they are soothing to young eyes. Pillows are best unpatterned, preferably in blue or soft green, to aid sleep. Nothing should be hung immediately over a sleeper's head, and bunk beds, although practical, are not beneficial to the child in the lower bunk, because the upper cot is oppressive to dreams. Toys, except cuddly ones, should be out of sight of beds, as they may be too stimulating.

Many children have a "spirit companion," whom we might assume is imaginary, but we can't be sure. If your child has an unseen playmate, make a special corner in the nursery for this friend.

While it is important to create a comforting, soothing atmosphere, don't forget your child may have been here before. When they are old enough to show preferences, consider placing safe adult items to which they have taken a fancy, in their rooms. For instance, a fascination with a Chinese painting or a carving of an Indian elephant could just mean your child has lived in the country. Try not to let your own bias intervene, but observe the child.

CHANGELING CHILDREN

Folk used to fear that fairies would take their child and leave in its place a "changeling." There are many spells to keep children safe from the little people, for fairies were often jealous of beauty or fell in love with it. One of the simplest ways to protect a child is to place daisies or peony roots around his or her crib. However, while fairies may be mischievous, we should seek to make friends with them, for they are the spirits of Nature from which we have become estranged.

Fairies inhabit Otherworld—that land that is so close to our own, but can only be glimpsed from the corner of the eye. Fairyland is another dimension, a part of the hidden spirit world, and far from being mere figments of childish fantasy, many peoples, ancient and modern, have had vivid experiences of its inhabitants. Fairies can be helpful and wise or puckish and troublesome—and it has long been believed that they have an affinity with children.

The Little Folk

There are many different orders of fairy. Some are mighty and powerful, others are smaller and more playful. Some are linked to specific plants and others are guardians of place, while some are elemental powers. The elemental spirits, according to folk tradition, are listed below.

ELEMENT	SPIRITS	TASK
Earth	Gnomes	Look after the soil and cherish minerals, crystals, and rock formations as well as plant life.
Air	Sylphs	Ride on the wind, tending trees, keeping the atmosphere clear and fresh.
Fire	Salamanders	Live in the heart of flames, giving them power.
Water	Undines	Dwell in lakes, rivers, waterfalls, and streams, blessing the water.

FAIRY BLESSING SPELL

Honor these elementals in the nursery by placing a ceramic pot of earth or a special stone in the north; wind-borne seeds or feathers in the east; a red candle in the south; and a chalice of water in the west. Do this at Full Moon. Starting in the north, ask first for the blessing of the gnomes, to give your child strength, protection, and practicality. In the east, ask for pure air to breathe and pure thoughts for the mind; in the south for vitality and imagination; and in the west, for love and understanding. Ask the gnomes, sylphs, salamanders, and undines for their special protection, and pledge to respect them and the natural world. Light a white candle to Queen Mab (who is yet another form of the Nature Goddess), asking her to watch over the cradle, and promise to do your best to bring up your child to honor all life.

Remove the earth, seeds, candle, and water from the nursery and relax in the knowledge that unseen powers are now protecting your child.

Bathtime Bliss

You may have little choice in regard to the layout of your bathroom, but you can work wonders creating an ambience there. Your bathroom offers fine opportunities to create a ritual setting, and bathtime gives you privacy and precious minutes to perform impromptu spells.

Remember the bathroom is a haven of sensuality, and meant for much more than just getting clean. Make sure that the lighting is subdued and the color scheme gives you a feeling of such warmth that when you take your clothes off, you are held in its embrace. Your bathroom is a celebration of your body, designed to make you feel gorgeous. A deep-pile rug, sumptuous robes and towels, and a thermostat turned up high will help you relax.

FABULOUS FRAGRANCE

Equip your bathroom with a selection of fragrances, from high-quality suppliers who use natural essential oils in their products. Store these in attractive colored jars, making a display for the light to play upon. Familiarize yourself with the effects of scents, for they evoke endless associations. Here is a small selection:

BERGAMOT is stimulating and bracing. Use it as an excellent pick-me-up when you feel sluggish.

EUCALYPTUS is a therapeutic scent with healing and decongestant properties. Eucalyptus oil or products including it can be sprinkled into bathwater, but be aware of the possibility of an allergic reaction.

LAVENDER is relaxing and soothing. It helps promote sleep but also clarifies the memory and can be erotic, too—especially to men, so tradition goes!

ORANGE is very stimulating and helps you to feel positive and optimistic (but orange essential oil may irritate the skin, so go carefully).

PATCHOULI is grounding and earthy. It will help you to be practical and realistic, but it can also be very lustful.

ROSE is associated with love and peaceful, close relationships. It is a great prelude to a romantic evening.

YLANG-YLANG helps release emotions, soothing feelings such as jealousy, and opening you to erotica.

CANDLE MAGIC

Candlelight reflected on water looks magical. Why not have row upon row of candles in many different colors, and a variety of holders (candelabra, lanterns, stained-glass crucibles), so that a multitude of flames dance in your bathwater?

BATHROOM GODDESS

Sulla was the ancient British goddess of hot springs and baths, and Aquae Sulis—the Roman name for the city of Bath, in Avon, England—was named after her. She was also goddess of the Sun. Sulla can be honored in your bathroom and asked for her blessing and healing. Use an emblem of the Sun (a sunflower or similar) or a suitable figurine to represent her. A lovely way to conjure Sulla is to light a floating candle in a solar color—gold or orange—and sail this in a bowl, the sink, or even on your bathwater, to warm and relax you, through and through.

Using the Element of Water

FROM WATER COMES ALL OF LIFE

The Koran

The element of Water offers a healing connection to all that has ever lived. Water nurtures, cleanses, and soothes. Water embraces and connects, flowing around and between. It symbolizes memories, tribal bonds, the ancestors, and traditions, for it changes, yet it is ever the same. It also transforms, for although its action is softer than that of Fire, it is relentless. Yet for all its power, Water runs away from between our fingers—it is subtle and changeable as the emotions.

Like Fire, Water inspires ritual, and the smallest thing we do with it can have symbolic meaning. Even filling a kettle with Water is part of a ritual welcome, as you start to brew tea. Every time we immerse our bodies in Water we are potentially performing a sacred act, for Water is a blessing. In the Chinese system of the elements, Water nourishes Wood, and so it is a wholesome statement to grow a plant in your bathroom—most plants love it and oblige by flourishing!

WASH YOUR WORRIES AWAY

Every bathtime can be turned into a spell if you are so inclined. Imagine that all your cares and worries, all those nasty feelings that you want to be rid of, are seeping out of you into the Water, settling downwards, so that when you pull the plug they all slip away. This is even better accomplished in a shower, where the Water runs away immediately. Your bath can also be used to absorb good things—for instance, strewing rose petals in your Water is a simple spell for beauty. For maximum effect, shower quickly first to rinse away negativity, and then luxuriate in a bath that you have symbolically saturated with your heart's desire.

Come on in, the Water's lovely!

BLOWING BUBBLES
(A Light-Hearted Spell)

Water symbolizes the emotions, and while the embrace of water can calm and reassure, if you have been very upset, disappointed, bitter, or bereft, a weighty feeling can linger even after many cleansing ceremonies.

Water is heavier than air, so bubbles are especially entrancing, because here the water is buoyed up by air—the water itself floats. Bubbles mean lifted spirits, giggles, pleasant trivia, and the easing of emotional loads.

All you need for your spell is your bathroom, lots of candles, some bubblebath (see box), and a bubble-blower from a child's bubble kit.

Have a shower using a little salt or lavender oil for extra cleansing. Name your particular problem and affirm that it is flowing away. Now light your candles and run a bath. Play music if you like, and enjoy the rush of water as it piles up the bubbles in frothy, glistening clouds.

When you are ready, lower yourself into the bath, equipped with your bubble-blower. Write symbols and messages with it in the froth. Play with the bubbles around you and blow the biggest ones you can, watching the shimmering globes carry your spirits up and up in the candlelight until they burst in a release of exciting energy that grows with each bubble. Imagine the bubbles carrying your wishes and dreams up into the air and releasing them into the atmosphere. You will have even more fun if you have a glass or two of wine on the side of the bath!

Carry on playing until the water goes cold and you long for your next treat—that velvety robe and sumptuous lotion that is waiting for you. The best things in life are often the simplest.

WHAT COLOR ARE YOU?

Wash away your troubles in bubblebath of an appropriate color. Use green for serenity, fertility, and money; pink for romance; or blue for clarity and freedom. See page 126 for more ideas.

Your Store-House

It is easy to forget your cellar or garage until you have to venture there to find something. However, this part of the house symbolizes your unconscious mind, the store-house of your experiences, the source of your impulses. If you have no cellar or garage, your cupboards take on this role. This is an important place.

STIR YOUR SUBCONSCIOUS

A fresh, tidy cellar signifies that you can face your unconscious, and that it is a fertile place. Don't leave junk here. Store wholesome root vegetables that smell of the earth, and stacks of wood or coal for burning. This is your powerhouse, your place of hidden riches that can be turned into something life-giving. Consecrate your cellar by lighting powdered incense or an incense stick of frankincense and myrrh, and moving it in a clockwise spiral while you imagine the air being freshened and creatively stirred.

Deep in your unconscious things are transformed, and if this is working healthily, yesterday's experiences become tomorrow's meanings. Make your cellar or cupboards a center for household transformation— here the recycling is tidily stored, with bulbs that will become plants and fuel that will become heat. It is a good idea to ferment wine or beer in your cellar, for this is a process of transformation, and the yeasty smell and the glug-glug from the demi-john will affirm to you each time you are there that something is stirring and growing. It's also a good place to germinate plants, store preserves to mature, and keep your racks of wine, bags of potatoes, and fragrant apples.

LORD OF THE UNDERWORLD

Here in your "Underworld" it is fitting to remember the Greek Underworld lord, Pluto. He was more than a god of the dead, he ruled the cycles of life and the seasons of nature, where the tomb becomes the womb. Pluto often wore a helmet of invisibility. He needs no pride of place but insists that you become part of his inexorable cycle. Show that you respect this by never avoiding your cellar or letting it stagnate.

Honor transmutation with a little Native American magic. Some traditions state that a shaman who wishes to turn into an animal can do so by wearing a chaplet of yucca fibers. Twist parts of a yucca plant—or substitute peppermint—into a circle, to hang in your cellar as a reminder that everything changes and there are more secrets in the universe than we can guess.

Your Head Space

If you have an attic, it represents your "head space"—your freedom to think, plan, recall, remake, and sort. Make sure it is not full of clutter, so the same thing cannot be said of your life! The loft is the place both for storage and inspiration. (If you have no loft, other parts of the house take on its function—probably upstairs cupboards.)

The attic is also a place of discovery, where you may find things to conjure with—old clothes for dressing up, a retro ornament that makes a statement tucked away in a niche, or even notes for the novel that you plotted out when you were seventeen. Your attic is the closest place in your home to the sky, and if your TV aerial is not within the loft, it will be nearby on the roof. Here you may catch some inspiration, as radio waves "earth" close by. Loft conversions are often used as studies so, if you have one, be aware of its exciting proximity to the sky, however you use the space.

LOFTY IDEALS

Be clear exactly what storage purposes your attic fulfills. It's the place for Christmas decorations, suitcases, temporarily unused furniture and appliances, and old schoolbooks that you love to leaf through occasionally. It is not the place for a broken iron or last year's junk mail—throw it out! Of course, you don't need to keep your loft as neat as your house, but maintain some order—memorabilia in one place, rarely used items in another.

MAKE YOUR OWN WORLD TREE

Shamanic cultures had a view of the cosmos as a World Tree, and a shaman who wished to travel in the Upper Worlds of spirit ascended this tree. The Norse name for this tree was Yggdrasil, and the ash was equated with it. If you wish to ascend spiritually when you go up to your loft, and tune in to the messages from the ether around you, you may like to feature ash here, perhaps as a staff. Twist an old wire coathanger into a circle and attach this to the top of the staff as an "aerial" of inspiration, for ash is a tree that connects disparate elements and is known to conduct lightning. Consecrate and bless your loft by taking burning powdered incense or an incense stick of sandalwood, frankincense, and/or lavender around it, moving the incense or incense stick in downward spirals to bring in fresh ideas from the sky-gods. Up, up—and away!

A Home for All Seasons

Off with the Old and On with the New

IT IS GOOD TO BE MERRY AND WISE,
IT IS GOOD TO BE HONEST AND TRUE,
IT IS BEST TO BE OFF WITH THE OLD LOVE,
BEFORE YOU ARE ON WITH THE NEW

ANON

Different cultures fix New Year in various months, but all over the world this is a time to get rid of the old and worn out, in order to make way for the new. The Western calendar sets New Year on January 1st—and what better time than deepest winter to start thinking about new life. After the hustle and bustle of the Christmas holiday season, it feels right to start on a new phase as we get back to normal and reorder our homes.

On New Year's Eve in Scotland, there is a custom of "first footing." It's said to be lucky if a dark-haired man or child is the first person to cross your threshold in the new year. They must bring a gift of coal or scotch.

THE KITCHEN GOD

Chinese New Year takes place at Full Moon in the beginning of February. In the week before New Year, Chinese families are especially careful to propitiate the Kitchen God Tsao Chun, because this is when he returns to heaven to file a report on the family. The Chinese burn paper effigies of him to speed his steps, with a little straw for his horse, and honey and alcohol to sweeten his tongue! Adapt this little ceremony for your own home, perhaps burning a paper Christmas lantern to bring your family a lucky new phase.

YOUR MIDWINTER ALTAR

The Celtic goddess Bride is remembered at the start of February. She was goddess of healing, smithcraft, poetry, childbirth, and creativity of all kinds. Sacred flames were kept alight in her honor and the snake, cow, bird of prey, and wolf were her animals— choose one of these for your altar. White candles and lavender oil are also suitable. In her honor, make a display of the family's creative efforts on a special noticeboard and shelf. Decorate the board and shelf in white, silver, and green, and wreathe them in holly and ivy. Take the sacred flame of the Bride from your altar and carry it ceremonially around the house when you decide your New Year begins.

TO DO

★ Throw out garbage and old linen
★ Give old clothes to charity

SILVER BELLS

Ring out the old and ring in the new with your own bells. Hang clusters of shining bells where you will brush them as you pass, place windchimes at every window and, however cold the weather, open the windows for a few minutes each day in early January and let the sharp, fresh air sweep in with a silvery melody.

Spring Cleaning

THE YEAR'S AT THE SPRING,
AND DAY'S AT THE MORN...
GOD'S IN HIS HEAVEN—
ALL'S RIGHT WITH THE WORLD!

ROBERT BROWNING, *PIPPA PASSES*

The fresh and hopeful air of spring makes us want to throw open windows and doors and invite in this new and wonderful power that makes the green shoots thrust and the flowers awaken. The growing Sun fingers dark and dusty corners, and it's natural to want to make our homes as sparkling as the season, literally and metaphorically. You could have an action replay of your initial cleansing ritual (see page 22), using a Native American sage and sweetgrass "smudge stick" instead of an incense stick, or try the lemon spell opposite.

Buy spring blooms such as daffodils and primroses for your windowsills. If your decor permits, reflect the season with yellow or bright green throws on beds and upholstery, and similar colors in tablecloths and napkins. Treat your house to a brightly colored vase or picture, and make or choose a lively window-sticker, to invite in the Sun.

YOUR SPRING ALTAR

Place bright yellow candles with bouquets of spring flowers or shamrock sprigs on your altar. You may want to give pride of place to a figurine of a spring goddess, a Celtic equal-armed cross, a nest with sugar eggs, or an Easter rabbit. Eggs are an ancient symbol of new life.

LEMON SPRING CLEAN

Make your home zing with this lemon spell. Peel three lemons over a bowl of warm water, so the peel falls in. Then squeeze the juice and flesh in, too. If possible, leave the lemon-water out in moonlight for a few hours before you use it.

Taking your chalice, scoop up a little of the mixture and drink a toast to the season with it. Say, **"May all be cleansed, within and without."** Find a pristine white cloth, dip it into the lemon-water, and lightly wipe around all your windowsills and door frames. Using your finger and thumb, flick a little of the water around each room and into the corners and cupboards. Don't worry about missing bits, because your intention is there. Imagine the freshness of the lemons leaving a subtle sparkle over everything in your home.

Empty out any remaining lemon-water onto the earth. Now spring has sprung within your home as well as outside. All things feel possible!

TO DO

★ Dust, polish, shine, sweep—clean your home from top to bottom

★ Buy spring flowers

★ Throw open your windows

Sensual Spring and Summer

WHEN BIRDS DO SING, HEY DING A DING, DING;
SWEET LOVERS LOVE THE SPRING

WILLIAM SHAKESPEARE, *As You Like It*

Of all the seasons, late spring is the most sensual. The air is heady with expectation, and life seems very sweet. It is a time to maximize sheer joy in living and to catch the moment within the pleasure zone of the home.

Many customs have fertility themes at the beginning of May, for agricultural communities sense this as summer's beginning. Going "a-maying" meant bringing in hawthorn, which was sacred to the Goddess of the Land. It is believed unlucky to have "the may" indoors before May 1st, because this pre-empts the natural cycle. Gathering hawthorn meant staying out all night beneath the stars, often resulting in "greenwood marriages" and a New Year baby.

YOUR MAY ALTAR

On your altar, place rose-colored candles and seasonal flowers.
A figure of the Faerie Queen (the original May Queen) or a magical dragon will speak of Earth-power.
A large crystal of rose quartz will enhance that loving vibe. Velvet heart-shaped cushions, a heart-shaped deep-pile rug, and some red lightbulbs will show that your home has love on its mind.

ROSES FOR LOVE

Repeat the spring cleaning lemon-water spell on page 105, but use rose petals instead. This time your intention is not to cleanse but to caress. Have a glass of your favorite tipple and play romantic music as you waft from room to room, sprinkling rose-water lightly around. In each room imagine delightful things happening, suitable to that part of the house. Dab the rose-water on your face as well, visualizing it adding to your attractiveness and making your skin glow. Make a gift of the remaining rose-water to your favorite plant. Feel the enchantment!

TO DO

★ Pamper yourself

★ Make love

★ Fill your home with the scent of spring flowers

For a traditional May, deck your home in white blossom, arranging lacy twigs in green vases and wreathing shelves and alcoves with delicate blooms. If you have less time—and don't want to cope with the mess of falling petals—use lace as a substitute. Drape your bedroom with lace and veils, turning it into a seductive haven.

Pay special attention to scent. Heat ylang-ylang or rose oil in your burner, fill vases with white roses or exotic lilies, or burn a sweet-smelling incense stick.

YOUR HIGH SUMMER ALTAR

Add red or green candles and bright flowers to your altar. Cretan New Year began at the summer solstice, so this is the time to display a bare-breasted Cretan priestess. In Ancient Crete, the humming of bees was believed to be the voice of the Goddess, so feature a bee figure, or fill your kitchen with honey products. Stones with naturally formed holes are thought lucky. Show them on your windowsill to recall the solstice alignment of Stonehenge.

Harvest Home

MISTY SUN AND STEAMING RAIN
UPON THE PREGNANT, SWELLING EARTH
DRYING TREES AND TIRING FIELDS
AWAIT THE MYSTERY OF BIRTH

Teresa Moorey, *Lammas*

At no time of year is it more evident that we depend upon Nature and her bounty than in late summer and at harvest-time. Your house wants to be part of this, to hold this richness and honor it, for its very walls are also a gift of the earth.

Buy scrumptious bread rolls and pile them in a basket in the kitchen. Feature flour and grains in chunky storage jars and keep chilled cider in a stout jug, to offer guests in earthenware chalices. Best of all, bake your own bread.

As the mellow Sun bends lower to reach through your window, heat frankincense oil in your burner and plan your creative projects for the coming months. Your house is the granary of your soul: as you sow, so you will reap.

YOUR LATE SUMMER ALTAR

Gold candles are appropriate for your altar now, and a bunch of poppies, ephemeral though they are, add a splash of color. Other suitable items are a pregnant goddess figure, a golden chalice (or anything made of gold or amber), or a sheaf of wheat. Bring splashes of gold and red into your home—gold daisies in a red pot, sunflowers, basketwork, red and amber stones grouped decoratively, brass artifacts, and figures made of glazed and hardened dough. Weave colored threads together to adorn shelves and banisters.

CORN DOLLY

There are many traditions connected with the harvest, one of the prettiest being the corn dolly. The spirit of the corn is kept alive in the dolly, which is made out of ears of wheat or wheat straw, and may be as complex as a human figure or simply a bunch of wheat. (Please note, "corn" here is wheat rather than maize, although a dolly can be made from corn husks, or oat and rye straw.) Red is the traditional color for the dolly's dress or the ribbon that ties the sheaf. Before harvest, go to a field of ripened wheat and pick a few stalks. Bind these together in your kitchen, imagining the generosity of the earth as you do so, and affirming that you are drawing this generosity to you, to keep, to enjoy, and to honor. I make a fresh corn dolly every year and hang it over my stove until the next one is ready to take its place, when I bury the old one. Your corn dolly is a potent good-luck charm for hearth or kitchen, and acts as a lovely, rustic reminder of the cycles of Nature in the modern home.

TO DO

★ Bake bread

★ Honor the goddess of the harvest

Autumn Preserves

**SEASON OF MISTS AND MELLOW FRUITFULNESS,
CLOSE BOSOM-FRIEND OF THE MATURING SUN**

JOHN KEATS, *TO AUTUMN*

At this time of year, mornings and evenings are hazy with the last breath of summer. Fields and forests are filled with Nature's harvest. In times past, preservation of foods for the winter was of the utmost importance in fall. Take the time to make your own preserves in acknowledgment of the fruitful season. Try pickling, making jam with late-summer fruits, or my delicious recipe for apple chutney (see box opposite).

Bring the riches of woodland into your home, maybe with images of mushrooms or arrangements of gorgeous fall leaves. Wooden mushrooms (found in craft shops) can be grouped cozily on shelves. The red-capped, white-spotted fly agaric is the most magical fungus. It's said that the shamans of the Russian steppes used the hallucinogenic properties of an ointment of fly agaric to make them "fly."

As the Sun slips lower in the sky, it's time to make sure the element of fire is making a strong showing in your house. Hang a Mexican "eye of

YOUR FALL ALTAR

Adorn shelves and your altar with sprigs of blazing leaves. Sycamore "wings," acorns, and other nuts are a reminder that nothing ever truly dies. Arrange them with care and joy. Stags are a potent link with the horned god of the woodland, so consider placing a figure of a stag or any other horned animal on your altar. Place candles of blackberry-purple on your altar and any gathering of wild bounty, such as rosehips and sloes. These can later be turned into preserves. The Egyptian God of the Dead, Osiris, will look majestic if figured on your altar, with his consort, the great Isis, as a tribute to the dying year.

APPLE CHUTNEY

I make this in autumn, when apples are plentiful. You will need 1 pound (450g) chopped onions, 1¼ cups (275ml) vinegar, 2 pounds (900g) unpeeled apples with good skins, cored and chopped, 6 tablespoons (75g) raisins, 1 teaspoon pickling spice in a cheesecloth or cotton pouch, 1 teaspoon ground ginger, 1 teaspoon salt, and 1⅔ cups (350g) soft brown sugar.

Put the onions into a pan with a little of the vinegar and simmer until soft. Add the apples, raisins, spices, salt, and enough vinegar to stop the mixture burning. Simmer until the apples are soft. Add the remaining vinegar and the sugar; boil until thick (15–20 minutes). Pour into warm, clean glass jars. Cover the lids with circles of bright fabric, secured by elastic bands. Display jars on shelves shaded from light.

light" (a colorful square, hung up by one corner, which symbolizes luck and harmony) in your hallway, to support the Sun's dwindling rays. If possible, have a real fire in your home, but if you can't, make sure there is a warm substitute to act as a focal point—a mock fire with a glowing bulb or a flamboyant arrangement of dried flowers in the grate.

Welcome winter, for your home is a shrine to enduring life.

TO DO

★ Make preserves

★ Decorate your home with Nature's bounty

★ Introduce the element of fire with bright colors or, best of all, a real fire

Spooks and Stories

**FROM GHOULIES AND GHOSTIES AND LONG-LEGGETY BEASTIES
AND THINGS THAT GO BUMP IN THE NIGHT,
GOOD LORD, DELIVER US!**

SCOTTISH VERSE

Outside the wind moans and the dried leaves dance like imps in the cold, gray air. Winter was a fearful time for our ancestors—not merely because the spirits of the dead walk at Halloween, but because vital decisions had to be made in order for the community to make it through to another spring. Nowadays, the only shivers we get are delicious, as we close our doors and savor the cheer and warmth of our homes.

Your home is eager to wrap you up against the chill and to remind you that just as life endures beneath the bare earth, so it is still vibrant between your walls. But it is good also to honor darkness, for it is part of life. So cut that leery eerie face in your pumpkin! Why not have several, one large one plus several smaller ones for each room, and one for your altar? Keep candles burning within, throughout the Halloween season, for these symbolize the secret continuity of life.

To the Celts, this was the start of the story-telling season, and in my family we set up the sitting room for a mini tribal gathering, with candles, books of ghost stories, and our talking stick (see page 37). Tradition goes that the person who holds the stick holds everybody's attention. Now we tell a round-robin Halloween ghost story that is often hilarious.

Ancestors were honored at this time, so give pride of place to photos of the dear departed in your family, surrounding them with candles, mementoes, and floral tributes. Heap scrumptious nuts in a bowl to nibble.

YOUR HALLOWEEN ALTAR

On your altar, place an effigy of Hecate, goddess of death and wisdom, or veil another goddess figure in black. Dare to have black candles, bats, and even a little witch flying from the ceiling by invisible thread! Place patchouli or myrrh in your oil burner for a heavy scent. If you have a cauldron, make a feature of it, filled with evergreen fronds, bought flowers, or some wonderful Chinese lantern (*Physalis alkekengi*) stems. The cauldron means transformation into new life, and by filling it with these plants you are conjuring something new and wonderful for your home.

Purchase special, bright, and comforting mugs to sip hot drinks by the fire. For once, why not leave your cobwebs in place—you could even feature them, sprayed with silver glitter, at your Halloween party! Indoor fireworks will add to the excitement.

Halloween was the Celtic New Year, for to the ancient Celts things began in darkness. We begin truly to appreciate our snug homes as winter approaches.

ALL SAINTS AND SOULS

The first and second of November are celebrated as "Days of the Dead" in Mexico. The souls of children are honored on November 1, All Saints' Day. Graves are cleaned and decorated with orange marigolds, white calla lilies, and bird of paradise flowers. Children give each other candies in the shape of skulls and skeletons, coffins and tombstones.

On the second of November, All Souls' Day, the recently deceased come to pay a visit to the living. They are welcomed back with special food left on the family altar. Macabre paper cut-outs are hung from altars and in public places.

TO DO

★ Decorate your home with carved pumpkins and lighted candles

★ Tell spooky stories

★ Honor your ancestors

Festive Household

**CHRISTMAS COMES BUT ONCE A YEAR
BUT WHEN IT COMES IT BRINGS GOOD CHEER**

16TH-CENTURY PROVERB

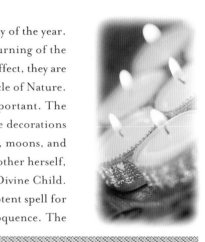

Christmas coincides with the winter solstice, the shortest day of the year. Most Christmas customs arose from a celebration of the turning of the year, bringing warmth and light into the dark of winter. In effect, they are all spells to ensure our safety and the continuation of the cycle of Nature.

The plants we bring into our homes at this time are important. The evergreen tree is a symbol of undying life. Choose your tree decorations with care, knowing that they are more than just pretty—suns, moons, and stars mean the cosmic cycle, the treetop fairy is the Holy Mother herself, the presents we give each other are a "baby shower" for the Divine Child.

Remember the mistletoe, for kissing underneath it is a potent spell for fertility—not just of the body, but of the mind, and for eloquence. The Druids cut mistletoe with a golden sickle in honor of Sun, Moon, and the process of birth, and it is believed to confer wisdom. Oak, ash, and birch are all said to have been brought in as the yule log—another symbol of ongoing life. A piece of each year's log was kept to kindle the next year's solstice flames. A small log holding a candle is a fine substitute—or you could indulge in the chocolate variety!

Observe the solstice by choosing a special colored candle for your windowsill and keeping it lit from December 21st until Christmas. For your oil burner, what better than frankincense oil, for its richness and majesty. Look out into the winter's night and imagine the secret life within the soil, sensing the first thrill of excitement at the Sun's return. Bless your home at Christmas and feel it respond with warmth and joy.

YOUR YULETIDE ALTAR

On your altar place candles of true red. Whatever your beliefs, feature a mother goddess with her child, for this wonderful birth links with the "rebirth" of the Sun. Why not have an entire crib, and place the new babe in his little straw bed late on Christmas Eve? Doing this honors the family, with the ox and ass as stolid representations of loyalty in the natural world. Wreathe your altar with holly and ivy, for traditionally these are "magical mates"—holly is male to ivy's female, and together they bring balance and blessing.

Moving On

Selling Your Home

A MAN'S HOUSE IS HIS CASTLE

SIR EDWARD COKE, *INSTITUTES*

When your house is on the market, you may feel insecure and that your destiny is in others' hands. A spell can help you regain control. First, however, work on your attitude to your home. If you have decided to sell, you may feel there are things wrong with it. Instead, try to remember what made you buy this home in the first place, all the good things about it and the happy times you have had there. Bring your lovely old home gifts such as a bunch of flowers or scented candles. Your attitude to your home will show unconsciously as you lead prospective buyers around, so be sure to fill your mind with happy memories at these times. Use photographs and mementoes to help you, if necessary. Then try this spell to get those contracts prepared in the subtle realms.

SALE AGREED

You will need some gum benjamin (or benzoin), cinnamon sticks, and dried basil (preferably dry some you have grown yourself). You will also need two green candles, an estate agent's picture of your house, a censer containing charcoal, and a red pen.

Make the benzoin, cinnamon, and basil into an incense by crumbling and mixing them, and as you do so imagine your old life in the house is going into the incense, to be transformed. Light your candles and place the picture of your house between them. Light your charcoal, and when it is sparking, sprinkle some of the incense into the censer. As you do so, imagine your house being sold, the telephone calls, the contracts, the moving arrangements. Waft the incense over the picture and write SOLD on it with the red pen, in bold letters. Now carry your incense over the entire house, loving it and imagining giving it over to someone else who will also love it. Place the picture, plus a little of the unburnt incense mixture, underneath your doormat. Sale agreed!

Finding A New Home

NOTHING SEEK, NOTHING FIND

16TH-CENTURY PROVERB

It's difficult to get what you want if you are not sure what that is! When you are looking for a new home, think about your priorities. What are the things you can't do without, and what could be adapted? Try to be realistic. When you are clear about what you want, you are ready to do your spell.

HOUSE-HUNTING SPELL

Go for a leisurely walk on which you are free to think and dream about your new home; so much the better if you can do this in the area you want to move to. Sniff the air, touch the trees, and imagine yourself also putting down roots where you want to be. As you walk, collect a stone for each of the rooms you'd like in your new home. Choose them for their color and shape—they should be roughly the same size. A blue one might symbolize your bathroom, an L-shaped one a living room of that shape, and so on.

Take your stones home and find a square green or brown scarf. You also need four brown candles—honey-color or dark green will do as a substitute—some patchouli oil, and green or brown string. Light the four candles around you, roughly to the north, south, east, and west. Face north with your scarf on your lap, a corner pointing towards each candle. Carefully anoint each corner with a little patchouli oil. Put your stones in the center of the scarf. Place your hands over them and imagine your new home as vividly as you can. When you are ready, wrap the stones carefully in the scarf and tie it with the string to form a pouch.

Keep your pouch somewhere safe and suitable—perhaps with your estate agents' leaflets. When you find your new home, give thanks and heat a little patchouli oil as you unwrap the pouch to take out the stones. Time for them to return to the earth. Plant them around your property or take them to parkland nearby. Now you are really settled in!

Moving Matters

As the day of your move approaches, it is natural to become a little anxious and to wonder if you are doing the right thing. Will the move be trouble-free? Will the family be happy in the new place? Your old home may suddenly seem very attractive and secure, and as you wander around familiar rooms, you may wonder if you are losing more than you are gaining. Perform this simple spell to ensure you are thinking positively and that everything of value will come with you, undisturbed, to your new abode.

HOME FROM HOME SPELL

Find a yellow or multi-colored scarf and some potpourri of a color to match. You also need a potpourri container that complements your new home, and which symbolizes something you value about it—perhaps space, if it is a large bowl; proximity to the country if it is green; and so on.

Ideally, all family members should take part in this spell. Spread the scarf on the dining table or anywhere the family gathers. Scatter the potpourri on the scarf. Everyone should hold their hands over the potpourri and think of all the qualities they most value about the current home and that they wish to take with them. Say these out loud if you wish. When everyone has finished, gather the potpourri up in the scarf and transport it with great care, along with the bowl, to the new place. As an extra, place comfrey leaves in your packing cases, for these are associated with safety while traveling. (You could put a comfrey leaf in your potpourri.)

When you are settled in your new home, carefully empty the potpourri into its new receptacle and bury the comfrey leaves in the garden. Place the bowl in the middle of the table and have a celebratory meal. All the good of your old home has come with you, in this bowl. At the end of the meal, place the bowl in a permanent home. Hang the scarf up in triumph—perhaps drape it over a picture, adding color to your room.

You'll feel as if you've lived there forever!

NEW HOME BLESSING

Once you have moved into your new home, you may not feel completely settled. You will want to make the place spiritually yours, as well as materially. In a sense, you need to woo the spirit of the place, for your home must want you as much as you want it. Give your new home the gift of a special blessing.

For this spell you will need a sprig of white heather or thyme. Heather is considered lucky, and thyme has the power to attract fairies. Fairies are Nature-spirits, and the goodwill of those who live close by can only be an advantage! You will also need a white, silver, or clear bowl or chalice, a silver candle in a silver holder, a basil leaf for each room, white wine, green grapes or white chocolate—and the light of the Full Moon.

Fill your bowl with water—preferably spring water—and leave it out in the moonlight for an hour or so. Place your "Moon-charged" water on a tray with the silver candle, the basil leaves, and the sprig of thyme or heather. Go from room to room in the darkness, by the light of your candle and the moonlight. Using the sprig of heather or thyme, sprinkle the moon-water lightly around each room, saying **"May my home be blessed, may the unseen powers welcome me as I do them, for the good of all, in the light of the Goddess."** Place a leaf of basil in each room, saying **"Herb of Mars, protect this room."** If you find it eerie to do this, have a companion. You may play soft music, if you wish.

When you have blessed each room, go out into the moonlight with your wine and sweet snack. Say, **"Great Mother, bless me and bless my house. Give me the wisdom and the serenity to make a secure and lovely home."** Toast Lady Moon with your wine and eat your snack in celebration of the gifts of life. (If the Moon goes in, don't worry, just do this by candlelight.) When you have finished, carefully pour the water from the chalice or bowl out onto the earth. Wear your sprig of thyme if you want to see fairies, or your heather for luck. Leave out some of the wine, and a snack on a white or silver plate, for the fairies. Old stories say that while they do not literally eat and drink, they absorb the essence of the offering with appreciation.

Now you have made friends with the neighbors!

TABLE OF MAGICAL CORRESPONDENCES

Material substances are connected with abstract purposes by a system of correspondences. Use these time-honored links in your own spells.

	PLANET	COLORS	SCENTS, INCENSE	GEMS, CRYSTALS	PLANTS, HERBS, SPICES	GODS, GODDESSES	OTHER
BEAUTY	Venus	blue, pink, rose	ylang-ylang	amber, opal, pearl	rose	Aphrodite, Freya	swans
CLEANSING	Moon	white	lavender, lemon	aquamarine	lavender, lemon	Vesta	besom, salt
COMFORT		orange, pink, red	camellia, sandalwood	carnelian	chamomile, cypress, lemon balm	Vesta	
CREATIVITY	Jupiter, Mercury, Venus	yellow	cinnamon, sandalwood	amber, sunstone, topaz	bay, carnation, hazel, orange, rosemary, sunflower	Apollo, Athena, Mercury	cauldron, chalice
DREAMS	Moon, Neptune	purple	lavender	amethyst	chamomile, lavender, rosemary	Hypnos, Morpheus, Selene	stars
FERTILITY	Moon	green	calamus, sandalwood	moonstone	sunflower, rice, wheat	Demeter	cauldron, chalice, eggs
FRIENDSHIP/ WELCOME	Jupiter, Venus	warm hues	lavender	pink tourmaline, turquoise	brown chrysanthemum, honeysuckle, lemon, passion flower, sweet pea	Lares, Jupiter	
HAPPINESS	Jupiter, Venus	brights, sparkly shades	lavender, lily of the valley	amethyst	hyacinth, lavender, lily of the valley, marjoram, St John's Wort	Kuan Yin	
HARMONY/ PEACE	Venus	blues, greens, lavender, natural shades, neutrals, soft pinks	jasmine, lavender, ylang-ylang	amethyst, aquamarine, blue tourmaline, lapis lazuli, obsidian, sapphire	jasmine, lavender	Kuan Yin	doves
HEALING	Moon	green	eucalyptus, lavender	amethyst, carnelian, diamond, garnet, holey stone	apple, lavender, lemon balm	Aesculapius, Apollo	crystal, pets
LOVE	Venus	blue, green, rose	jasmine, lavender	amber, amethyst, lapis lazuli, moonstone, sapphire	jasmine, lavender, thyme	Aphrodite, Eros, Isis	heart shapes
LUCK	Jupiter	purple	clove	alexandrite, aventurine, holey stone	daffodil, honeysuckle	Fortuna	horseshoe, star
MONEY	Venus	green	jasmine, patchouli	emerald, pearl, ruby	almonds, basil, cinnamon, clove, dill, honeysuckle, jasmine, oak	Mercury (trade), Venus	coal
NOURISHMENT	Moon	apricot, cream, orange, peach		moonstone, topaz	wheat	Demeter	Green Man
PRIVACY	Saturn	black, brown, dark blue	myrrh	geodes, sodalite	yew	Lares	
PROSPERITY	Jupiter, Sun	gold, purple	cinnamon, frankincense	marble	cinnamon, nuts, oak, sage	Fortuna, Jupiter	
PROTECTION	Mars, Saturn	black, brown, dark blue, dark green	myrrh, patchouli	carnelian, garnet, red tourmaline	basil, bay, cactus, chrysanthemum, geranium, hawthorn, holly, hyacinth, marigold, primrose, rowan	Artemis, Athena, Cernunnos, Mars, Saturn	
RELAXATION		blues, greens, lilac	lavender	kunzite	chamomile, lavender		
SENSUALITY	Venus	black, deep red, rose pink	patchouli, ylang-ylang	garnet, ruby	cinnamon, mint, rosemary	Aphrodite, Freya	

PICTURE CREDITS

All photography by Emma Lee, with styling by Finola Inger, except as stated below

KEY: a=above, b=below, r=right, l=left, c=center

Caroline Arber 14, 15, 50–51, 93r

Henry Bourne 17r, 104–105, 107ar

Martin Brigdale 102r

David Brittain 12, 45r, 58–59, 62–63, 109, 110c, 112, 113l, 115

Christopher Drake 28l & 29b designer Barbara Davis' own house in upstate New York, 30l Jonathan and Camilla Ross' house in London, 31l Marisa Cavalli's home in Milan, 55ar

Melanie Eclaire 28–29 Sarah Raven's Cutting Garden in Brightling, designed by Sarah Raven, 29ar

Chris Everard 49 main, 98–99 Jo Warman—Interior Concepts

Catherine Gratwicke 13, 36c, 37c, 44al, 44bl an apartment in Paris designed by Bruno Tanquerel, 52–53, 77 Bryan Purcell, an artist living in New York, 110al, 113r

Sandra Lane 102l, 103r, 114

Tom Leighton 18l

William Lingwood 22ar, 61, 102–103

Ray Main 19l, 52l, 98b a house in Paris designed by Hervé Vermesch, 99al David Mellor's home and studio at Hathersage in Derbyshire, 99ar

Marianne Majerus 57br

James Merrell 10r, 16, 19r, 21, 22br, 37l, 54br, 59, 66bl Amy and Richard Sachs' apartment, New York (design Vicente Wolf), 72r, 96a, 96–97, 98a, 108al, 110bl & ar, 111r

David Montgomery 6, 7, 12–13, 17l, 22l, 23, 50l, 56, 57a & bl, 76, 82–83 background, 83l, 92–93, 105r, 108b

Craig Robertson 111l

Debi Treloar 44–45, 58a, 65bl Robert Elms and Christina Wilson's family home in London, 65br Jill Henry and Jon Pellicoro's family home in New York, 87–88 (87l & 87–88 the Boyes' home in London designed by Circus Architects, 88ar Pear Tree Cottage, Somerset, mural by Bruce Munro)

Pia Tryde 11l, 96b, 97b

Chris Tubbs 10l, 11r, 36l & 38 a cottage in Connecticut designed by Bernard M. Wharton, 36r a house in Ramatuelle, St. Tropez, 48, 49 inset, 60, 64, 94

Alan Williams 97a

Andrew Wood 30r Charlotte Crosland Interiors, 37r, 50r Jane Collins of Sixty 6 in Marylebone High Street, home in central London, 54–55 Sally and Ian's home in England, 66–67 Ian Bartlett and Christine Walsh's house in London, 92l

Polly Wreford 20 Daniel Jasiak's apartment in Paris, 20–21, 31r Ros Fairman's house in London, 40–41, 54l, 55bl Ann Shore's former house in London, 65ar, 71 Ann Shore's former house in London, 72l Mary Foley's house in Connecticut, 73, 82l, 82–83c, 83r, 92c, 104l, 106–107

STOCKISTS

Sixty 6
t. +44 20 7224 6066
Vintage furniture, clothes, and accessories

Story
t. +44 20 7377 6377
Personal selection of old and new furniture and accessories. Appointment only

BUSINESS CREDITS

Marisa Tadiotto Cavalli
t. +39 03 48 41 01 738
f. +39 02 86 46 24 26
marisacavalli@hotmail.com
Page 31l

Charlotte Crosland Interiors
t. +44 20 8960 9442
Page 30r

Circus Architects
t. +44 20 7953 7322
f. +44 20 7953 7255
Pages 87l & 87–88

Barbara Davis
t. 607 264 3673
Interior design, antique hand-dyed linen, wool, and silk textiles by the yard, soft furnishings, and clothes to order
Pages 28l & 29b

Interior Concepts
t. +44 20 8508 9952
f. +44 20 8502 4382
www.jointeriorconcepts.co.uk
Pages 98–99

Daniel Jasiak, Designer
t. +33 1 45 49 13 56
f. +33 1 45 49 23 66
Page 20

Nicoletta Marazza, Interior Designer
t. +39 02760 14482
Page 36r

David Mellor Design
t. +44 1433 650 220
f. +44 1433 650 944
davidmellor@Ukonline.co.uk
Page 99al

Bruce Munro
Mural commissions
t. +44 1749 813898
brucemunro@freenet.co.uk
Page 88ar

Jon Pellicoro, Artist
mhfny@inch.com
Page 65br

Rebecca and Bryan Purcell, Artists
436 Fort Washington Avenue
New York NY 10033
Page 77

Sarah Raven's Cutting Garden
t. +44 1424 838181
f. +44 1424 838571
www.thecuttinggarden.com
Pages 28–29

Ann Shore
London-based designer and stylist. Owner of Story
t. +44 20 7377 6377
Pages 55bl, 71

Bruno Tanquerel, Artist
t. +33 1 43 57 03 93
Page 44bl

Bernard M. Wharton
Shope Reno Wharton Associates
t. 203 869 7250
www.shoperenowharton.com
Pages 36l & 38

Christina Wilson, Interiors Stylist
christinawilson@btopen world.com
Page 65bl

Hervé Vermesch
t. +33 1 42 01 39 39
Page 98b

Vicente Wolf Associates, Inc.
333 West 39th Street
New York NY 10018
Page 66bl

INDEX